Dressed for the Business at Hand

A Study on the Spiritual Armor of God

Jodie Sewall

Thank-you Nancidee for the privilege of studying this with you and for the insights you offered to me. May you experience God's all-sufficiency and may you always have a willing spirit to follow where He leads you. Thank you also to the ladies at First Baptist Church in New Port Richey, FL and the staff ladies at Word of Life Florida who studied this with me and helped to refine this important study! May God be seen in you as you clothe yourselves in the armor of God. Many thanks also to Leslie Fisher for helping me to edit this document. Your help will keep the readers from being distracted by all my typing errors! I am so thankful for your help!

Dressed for the Business at Hand
A Study on the Spiritual Armor of God
2012

Sewall Publishing

ISBN: 978-0-578-11539-9

All Rights Reserved

Printed in the United States of America

Unless otherwise noted, all Scripture quotations are taken from the Holman Christian Standard Bible® Copyright © 1999, 2000, 2002, 2003 by Holman Bible Publishers. Used by permission. Holman Christian Standard Bible®, Holman CSB®, and HCSB® are federally registered trademarks of Holman Bible Publishers.

THE HOLY BIBLE, NEW INTERNATIONAL VERSION®, NIV® Copyright © 1973, 1978, 1984, 2011 by Biblica, Inc.™ Used by permission. All rights reserved worldwide.

Table of Contents

What Should I wear? --- 3

Homework Lessons - Belt of Truth --- 8

The Belt Modeled by the Savior --- 27

Homework Lessons - Breastplate of Righteousness --- 31

A New Heart --- 51

Homework Lessons - Feet Sandaled with Readiness for the Gospel of Peace --- 55

Forgiven Feet are Obedient Feet --- 71

Homework Lessons - Shield of Faith --- 75

"Come" --- 91

Homework Lessons - Helmet of Salvation --- 97

"I'm willing, can he come too?" --- 117

Homework Lessons - Sword of the Spirit --- 122

Unsheathed, the Sword is a life-changer! --- 139

∞∞∞∞∞

The Armored Baton – A resource for parents & grandparents --- 145

Introductory Lesson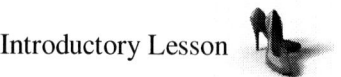

What Should I Wear?

"What should I wear?"

We ask this question every day. We evaluate our day, and, based on what we're going to be doing, where we're going, etc., we pick the right outfit to wear because as women we know how important it is to be dressed appropriately for the day and its events!

We understand the importance of dressing appropriately; we wouldn't wear a dress on a hunting trip or our ratty, old paint clothes to a friend's wedding. I am wondering if you know that God's Word has something to say about being dressed appropriately too.

The book of Ephesians tells us a lot about how we should be dressed spiritually. There are qualities in our lives that we should "put off" and other qualities that we should "put on." It also gives us a description of a spiritual suit of armor!

Let's take a quick overview of this book to discover what we should be wearing spiritually and why. This overview will create a foundation for our in-depth, piece-by-piece study of the armor of God mentioned in Ephesians, chapter six.

The book of Ephesians is six chapters long and is easily divided into two clear sections of teaching. The first three chapters are theology, and the last three are the practical application of that theology. I have heard the first three chapters described as **who we are-in Christ** and the last three chapters as **how we live-in Christ.**

Another teacher described the first three chapters as **the believer in Christ** and the last three chapters as **Christ in the believer**.

We must understand **who we are** before we can understand **what we do**.

After we have been changed by God and given the Spirit of Life and Light, we will live differently than before. Our position has changed; we were dead and now we are alive. Now we act like people who are alive, people who have the Life of God in them. We are in Christ now, and because we are in Christ, we live like Christ.

The world gets this mixed up, and sometimes Christians do too. They think if they act a certain way they will be changed. This is a works-based theology and is contrary to what the Bible teaches. We simply cannot earn a position in Christ. It is His gift to us. That is, His grace.

Our position has radically changed. I am reminded that our salvation is a bit like Disney's Cinderella story, except that little Cinderella has some redeeming qualities that make her attractive to the Prince. We cheer when the Prince rescues her because we know that she deserves a better life. God's love story toward us is even more radical; it would be like the

Prince choosing one of the wicked step-sisters to be His bride. Shocking! She doesn't have any redeeming qualities! She is ugly inside and out. She is mean-spirited, wicked, selfish, and she doesn't deserve the Prince. Hollywood wouldn't write this type of Cinderella story because we wouldn't like it. It doesn't seem right. That, my friend, is God's amazing love story toward us. The Son chooses us, not because we are beautiful and worthy, but because as He changes us, we showcase His rich grace. He saved us because of His grace, not because of any works that we did to earn His favor (Ephesians 2:3-9).

Saved by God's grace, we don't have any reason to boast about our salvation--We had nothing to do with it. We were dressed in filthy rags of righteousness, pursuing the lusts of our flesh. We had nothing good within us; we were dead and without the life of God. Then along came God's grace. He offered us His gift of Jesus Christ. We believed and we were saved. God put His Spirit within us as a down payment. We belong to Him now. We are his beloved bride; we are His church, His body, for the praise of His Glory (Ephesians 1:11-14; Ephesians 2:1-9)!

Ephesians 2:10 For we are His creation, created in Christ Jesus for good works, which God prepared ahead of time so that we should walk in them.

What good things does God have planned for us to do?

- He is changing us; we are being transformed into his image. We are becoming more like God. Our family resemblance is growing. Each day we have the opportunity of allowing God to do a good work in us!
- God wants us to show the sin-darkened world around us what the God of Glory is like. Everyday God gives us opportunities to show other people what He is like.

This is a summary of the works that God has planned for us to do. These are His goals for each one of us. How will He accomplish those works in and through us? God is very detailed and specific in His plan to transform each one of us. He will be at work individually sculpting each one of us. He will be chiseling away everything that doesn't look like Him. I may need more work in some areas than you do, and you may need more work in other areas. My path to sanctification will look different than yours will.

But if the work that God wants to accomplish through our lives is that we would show Him to the world around us, then I suggest that we all need to be "revealing" the same God, right? If we have been charged with the opportunity to imitate God, to be his representative here on Earth, we should have a lot of similarities in our behavior because we are all representing the same God!

Ephesians 4:4-6 There is one body and one Spirit —just as you were called to one hope at your calling— [5] one Lord, one faith, one baptism, [6] one God and Father of all, who is above all and through all and in all.

He should be represented the same way.

Introductory Lesson

Ephesians 4:1 Therefore I, the prisoner for the Lord, urge you to walk worthy of the calling you have received. Ephesians 5:1-2 Therefore, be imitators of God, as dearly loved children. ² And walk in love, as the Messiah also loved us and gave Himself for us, a sacrificial and fragrant offering to God.

Ephesians, chapters four, five, and six give us instruction about how to live in a manner that represents God. We are given contrasting commands of how not to live and then how we should live. If we are representing God, then we need to make sure that we are living a true representation of Him.

Ephesians 4:17-31 reminds us that in our new position, we shouldn't think and act like we did before we came to know God, and we are given a whole list of qualities that we are told to put off. Like taking a soiled garment off, we are to take these unholy characteristics off and clothe ourselves in Christ-likeness.

We are told to no longer walk as the Gentiles do. We should rid ourselves of these qualities:

Callousness (4:19)
Promiscuity (4:19)
Impurity (4:19)
Deceitful desires (4:22)
Lying (4:25)
Anger (4:26)
Stealing (4:28)
Rotten talk (4:29)
Bitterness (4:31)
Anger (4:31)
Wrath (4:31)
Brawling (4:31)
Slander (4:31)
Wickedness (4:31)
Sexual Immorality (5:3)
Impurity (5:3)
Greed (5:3)
Foolish talk/foolish living (5:4; 5:17)
Coarse joking (5:4)
Drunkenness (5:18)

We don't want to be a Cinderella who refuses to change. Can you imagine her living in the palace, her position having been changed, but insisting on wearing her old, ragged clothes and refusing to be transformed? She would still be a princess, but she would be a poor representative of the Prince and his provisions for her.

Interspersed in these chapters is another list, qualities representing God that should be present in our lives. These are the characteristics that we are told to "put on." We take off our old sinful ways and we are to "put on" Christ-likeness.

We are told to put on:

Humility (4:2)
Gentleness (4:2)
Patience (4:2)
Forbearance (4:2)
New mind (4:23)
Our new man created in God's likeness righteousness and truth (4:24)
Speak truthfully (4:25; 5:9)
Resolve issues (4:26)
Honest work (4:28)
Talk that builds up others (4:29)
Kindness (4:32)
Compassion (4:32)
Forgiving (just like Christ) (4:32)
Self-sacrificing (5:2)
Thankfulness (5:4; 5:20)
Goodness (5:9)
Righteousness (5:9)
Wise living (5:15)
Speaking to one another in Psalms, hymns, and spiritual songs (5:19)
Submitting to one another out of reverence to Christ {Husbands, wives, children, parents, employees, employers}(5:21 -6:9)

When we live with these characteristics present in our lives, we are representing God to others. The Glory of God is seen in our lives. We are allowing God to perform a transforming work in our own lives, and in doing so, our extreme make-over reveals God to others.

God has planned works for us to do. He wants us to be more like Him and He wants us to show others what He is like. That is God's will for us!

Ephesians 5:15-17 Pay careful attention, then, to how you walk—not as unwise people but as wise— [16] making the most of the time, because the days are evil. [17] So don't be foolish, but understand what the Lord's will is.

God's plan to accomplish these works in our lives is personalized; it is different for you than it is for me. He will use different people, different circumstances, different trials, etc. God has promised that He will complete the good work that He began in us (Phil. 1:6).

Introductory Lesson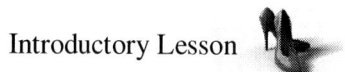

Paul has a warning for us!

Ephesians 6:10-12 introduces us to an enemy who is at work against us. Satan doesn't want us to look any more like God and he certainly doesn't want anyone else to see what God is really like. He is going to try to stop us. We are told in these verses that we are going to be engaged in warfare, personal attacks against us. Satan wants us to live like we did when we were dead in our trespasses and sins. He wants us to live with darkened thinking, fulfilling the lusts of our flesh and conforming to the world. If we live like that, we won't be changed to look like God, and other people will never get to see God revealed in our lives.

God has great works for us to do, and Satan is scheming to defeat us. Paul takes the time to warn us about our enemy and then he gives us the great news that we have been given the necessary tools to protect ourselves from Satan's plan for evil in our lives. We have battle gear – a suit of armor – spiritual armor that will protect us from the influences of Satan that would prohibit us from completing the works that God wants to accomplish in and through our lives.

Paul is telling us that we are going to be engaged in warfare and he tells us the specific pieces we need to wear. If we want to live wisely, we will make sure that we have clothed ourselves in the pieces that have been made available to us. We want to be dressed for success; we want to be dressed for the business at hand so that we can accomplish the works that God has prepared for us. If we ignore this spiritual armor, we foolishly make ourselves vulnerable to the attacks of the devil, and instead of completing the works that God has planned for us, we will experience defeat.

Over the next six weeks, we will study Ephesians 6:10-18. Begin now to ask God to teach you new truths about the armor of God. Pray that these truths will change your life. As you study each piece of armament, you will find yourself being strengthened in the Lord. By the time we finish our study, you will be dressed for the business at hand because you will be clothed in the armor of God, strengthened by the Lord.

You can be sure that Satan will do everything in his power to convince you that you do not have the time to complete an in-depth study of God's Word. Don't believe the lie. He does not have your best interests in mind (See page 147).

God does have your best interest in mind and He wants you live an abundant life!

Ephesians 2:10 For we are His creation, created in Christ Jesus for good works, which God prepared ahead of time so that we should walk in them.

If you have children, plan to also read the introductory lesson of *The Armored Baton* (page 145).

Week 1
The Belt of Truth

Day 1: We Need the Armor

Day 2: The Importance of the Belt

Day 3: Have You Misplaced Your Belt?

Day 4: Warfare with the Belt

Day 5: The Belt in Place

Lesson 1

We Need the Armor

**The LORD is my light and my salvation— whom should I fear?
The LORD is the stronghold of my life—of whom should I be afraid? Psalm 27:1**

This study is on the spiritual armor of God described in Ephesians, chapter six. As we study God's word, we will discover that He has given us everything we need for life and godliness through our knowledge of Him who called us (2 Peter 1:3).

Ephesians 2:1-3 describes three forces that war against the things of God: our fallen world, the devil, and our sinful nature. Before we knew Jesus as our Savior, we were in bondage to those sinful slave drivers, but verses 4 and 5 continue with, **But God, who is rich in mercy, because of His great love that He had for us, ⁵ made us alive with the Messiah even though we were dead in trespasses. You are saved by grace!** We were lost and our condition was hopeless until God, because of his great love for us, made us alive with Christ. I love that!

Our position before God has been changed; now we stand before Him forgiven, having received His grace. Verse 10 explains that as recipients of God's grace we are God's "creation." In the Greek the word translated *creation* is the word *poiema* from which we derive our English word *poem*. Isn't that beautiful? Can you picture God laboring over our lives, shaping it and creating it into His beautiful image? His work in our lives has purpose, shape, and form. The rest of that verse says **For we are His creation, created in Christ Jesus for good works, which God prepared ahead of time so that we should walk in them.**

Ephesians, chapters four, five, and six instruct the believer how to live like the "creation" of God. We still live in a fallen world, we still live in a body that craves the things of the flesh, and we still face the devil who rules the demonic forces in this present world. But God has provided everything we need to live godly lives. The truths about the armor of God that Paul gives us in verses 13-18 will help us live as God's creation in whatever situation we face, whether a temptation from the world, our sinful flesh, or a scheming attack from the devil.

We begin our study by taking a few minutes to identify our enemy. Scripture gives us many insights into how our enemy thinks and behaves, and we are going to look up some passages that identify his characteristics and tactics.

Ephesians 6:10-13 Finally, be strengthened by the Lord and by His vast strength. ¹¹ Put on the full armor of God so that you can stand against the tactics of the Devil. ¹² For our battle is not against flesh and blood, but against the rulers, against the authorities, against the world powers of this darkness, against the spiritual forces of evil in the heavens. ¹³ This is why you must take up the full armor of God, so that you may be able to resist in the evil day, and having prepared everything, to

take your stand.

We learn from these verses that the enemy is making plans against us and we will struggle against him. He has power, and there are other evil beings who work with him. One fact about him in this passage that I don't want you to miss is that he is defeatable! We are told that we will face the enemy in battle, and it will be a struggle. But in the end we can be standing.

Look up the following verses and record your observations about the enemy. How does he think? What kind of tactics does he employ? Who does he target? What are his goals? When you have completed this assignment, you will have a greater understanding of why we have been given spiritual protection.

I Peter 5:8 _____

The word *adversary* in the Greek means against a cause. [1] The devil is against the cause of man and he will do everything he can to destroy us. The word *devil* in the Greek means one who falsely accuses and divides people without any reason, one who casts either himself or something between two in order to separate them, false accuser. [2] The devil divides and he will do whatever he can to destroy the relationship we have with Christ. His goal is to drive a wedge of sin between us and God. He is full of hate, and we are the targets of his hatred.

II Corinthians 2:10b-11 _____

Unconfessed sin gives Satan an upper hand in his plotting against us. He looks for ways to take advantage of us. We need a heightened awareness that he is always planning and thinking against us.

II Corinthians 11:2-3 _____

The devil uses trickery and is cunning. The definition of the Greek word for *cunning* includes the idea of using subtle reasoning and craftiness.[3] Because the enemy attacks with subtlety and craftiness, one of the dangers is that we won't recognize his presence.

II Corinthians 11:13-15 _____

He may come disguised as an angel of light which means that he will present himself to us as something that looks good. One defense we have against this form of deceit is to know the genuine Angel of Light so well that the imitation angel will be exposed immediately!

Knowing that we have an enemy and that he roams around trying to destroy us should create an

---

[1] Zodhiates, Spiros, ed. *The Hebrew-Greek Key Word Study Bible* (Chattanooga, TN: AMG Publishers, 1996) #476, page 1806

[2] Ibid, #1228, page 1821

[3] Strong, James, *A Concise Dictionary of the Words in the Greek Testament* (Nashville, TN Abingdon Press, 1890) #3834, page 54

The Belt of Truth | Week 1

urgency to be spiritually prepared for the attacks. If God desires that we live spiritually victorious lives and has equipped us with everything we need to complete the works that He has prepared for us to do, why is it that many Christians find this victorious life elusive?

They experience defeat because they have not dressed for the right occasion—spiritual warfare. We need to recognize that spiritual battles are a reality for Christians and we need to be dressed appropriately to defend against them.

How can we live victoriously in this world?

Ephesians 6:10-12 Finally, be strengthened by the Lord and by His vast strength. ¹¹ Put on the full armor of God so that you can stand against the tactics of the Devil. ¹² For our battle is not against flesh and blood, but against the rulers, against the authorities, against the world powers of this darkness, against the spiritual forces of evil in the heavens.

Be strong in the Lord and in His mighty power.

The strength and power to prevail against the enemy will come from God, not from us. If we place our confidence in our own strength and power, we will be very much like the Israelites, who, in their own strength and power, cycled in and out of sin for forty years in the wilderness.

I Corinthians 10:11-13 tells us that the Israelites' struggle and their repeated failures came because they became confident in their own strength. God has ordained that no circumstance or situation will come into our lives that will bring a temptation greater than we can withstand because with each temptation comes the protection of God, a way of escape. This protection becomes available to us as we look to God for His power and strength.

In Ephesians 3:16, how will we be strengthened? _through the H.S. in the inner man_

What does II Peter 1:3 tell us that we have been given? _things that pertain to life and godliness through the knowledge of Him_

His divine power has given us everything we need to live godly lives. The word *life* in II Peter 1:3 is the Greek word *zoe*, and it means spiritual life. It is greater than the word *bios* which means physical life. This spiritual life that we have been given is the highest and the best kind of life which Christ has to give.[4] When we accept Christ as our Savior, God's divine Spirit comes and dwells within us. On our own, we don't have strength or power to fight against the evil one, yet if we rest in God and in His strength and power, we will have all that we need to be victorious. I am so thankful for this knowledge.

---

[4]Zodhiates, Spiros, ed. *The Hebrew-Greek Key Word Study Bible* (Chattanooga, TN: AMG Publishers, 1996) #2222, page 1838

Dressed for the Business at Hand

Wear the spiritual armor that God has provided.

According to Ephesians 6:11, how do we get strong in Him and in His mighty power? _by putting on the whole armor of God_

The key word in that phrase is *full*. We can sometimes find ourselves outfitted in only a partial suit of armor, and when that happens, we are vulnerable to the enemy's attacks. Strength and power come to us when we are fully clothed in the armor of God.

Read Ephesians 6:13 again. Does this verse say **if** the day of evil comes or **when** the day of evil comes? _that you may be able to withstand in the evil day_

What is the difference between these two words? _When = being able to resist_

The Word of God makes it clear that there is an enemy and we will face him.

What encouragement does this verse offer about the result of our encounter if we have clothed ourselves in the armor of God? _We are to stand_

How do we face him and come out still standing? We apply verses 11 and 13 in our life. In the strength and power of God, we put on the full armor of God.

In order to put on the full armor of God, we are going to need to know what the full armor of God is.

Dress Check:
Thankfully, we can claim **I John 4:4 . . . the One who is in you is greater than the one who is in the world.** How does this verse comfort you or give your courage to face each day? _I am an overcomer because I am in Christ and He is greater, who is alive in me. The one who is in the world (Satan) is not a match with the great I AM — Christ in me and I in Christ._

Take a few moments to pray and ask God to enable you to understand the spiritual armor as you study it. I love to pray Ephesians 3:14-21. I think it would bless your heart to pray it also.

We know that we have passed from death to life. If our heart condemns us, God is greater than our heart and knows all things. If our heart does not condemn us we have confidence toward God.

Lesson 2

The Importance of the Belt

You will know the truth, and the truth will set you free. John 8:32

I chuckle as I read the title I gave to this lesson. For my son, Tom, a belt was an important piece of his wardrobe; if he didn't wear a belt, he'd lose his pants before he walked ten steps. In my particular case, however, a belt is just an accessory. My blue jeans are not in any danger of falling off. I hope you chuckle with me on that. The belts used by men who lived in biblical times were not decorative; they served an important function.

Read each of the Old Testament passages below and describe the basic purpose of the belt in each instance.
Exodus 12:11 _the LORD's passover - getting ready to leave_
I Kings 18:46 _Elijah - girded up his loins to run ahead of Ahab_
II Kings 4:29 _____
II Kings 9:1 _getting ready to go to Gilead_

Cloaks were tucked into the belt. These passages also describe an action that occurred after the cloaks were tucked into the belts. What was the action? _to run - to move quickly_

The thought here is that you can move quickly once you have tucked your garment into the belt. Can you picture a group of people, as the case was in Exodus, or individual men as in the other passages, trying to run or make haste in long flowing robes? Picture with me that as you lean forward to run your robe begins to drag on the ground in front of you and your steps become hampered as you try not to step on your robe. A belt was a necessity if you wanted to move ahead with speed and certainty.

When the Apostle Paul described the belt of truth in Ephesians six, people would have understood this concept because they too wore long robes. They would have also pictured the Roman soldiers who walked around their towns. A belt was part of the standard equipment issued to a soldier. The belt held the pieces of armor together in an orderly fashion. Without a belt, a soldier would not have been considered properly dressed. In II Timothy 2:3, Paul makes the point clear that we have all been called to be soldiers for Christ Jesus. If our "belt of truth" is missing, we too are considered improperly dressed.

We explored the necessity of a belt, but what does it mean to have a belt of truth? Let's see what God's Word teaches about truth; then we will put the two together.

Look up Psalm 31:5. How is the LORD God described? _the LORD God of truth_

Dressed for the Business at Hand

According to John 14:6, who is truth? __Jesus__

John 14:17 gives us a descriptive name of the Holy Spirit of God. What title is He given in this verse? __the Spirit of truth__

As we study and know our God in all three persons of the Godhead, there is truth. God is truth.

Over 80 different times in the Gospel accounts, Jesus assured the people He was speaking the truth to them. In the KJV, you will find the words "Verily, Verily." In the NIV it is translated, "Truth, I am speaking truth to you." In the Holman Christian Standard, it is "I assure you."

Why do you think it was important that Jesus emphasized that **His** words were truth? __By knowing the truth we come to know Jesus as Messiah — the truth of who He was__

The priesthood had failed in their responsibility to teach the pure truth of God's Word. The traditions and additional commands they had burdened the people with had clouded their minds so that the Jewish people didn't even know what the truth was. They had been following what they believed to be the truth, but they were not being led to God. Jesus, the long-awaited Messiah, had now come and He began to teach them the truth of the Old Testament, the truth of God, and the truth of who He was. He repeated "Truth, I speak Truth" so many times in order that people would begin to alter their thinking by discerning the truth and begin to follow Him.

Let that sink in. He is TRUTH. I looked up the word *truth* in Webster's dictionary and the definition states, "faithful; the state of being the case; fact; it may represent a quality of statements, acts, or feelings of adhering to reality and avoiding error or falsehood." I am particularly drawn to the last phrase because it means that truth keeps us from error.

Look up John 8:31-32. What does Jesus say will set men free? __the Truth (Jesus)__

What was the truth (vs. 31)? __His Word__

Look up John 17:13-19. In this precious passage recording the prayer that Jesus Christ prayed on the eve of His crucifixion, what does Jesus say is truth (vs. 17)? __the Word of God is truth — the truth sanctifies the believer__

Ephesians 6:14 instructs us to stand firm with the belt of truth buckled around our waist. We are to know the Word of God. The belt of truth is the first piece of armor that we need to put on. Knowing God's Word is imperative if we want to move forward, prepared for whatever spiritual battles we will face. Without the belt of truth, we will be unsure of our step, hesitating, and being deceived along the way and we will become easy targets to the enemy.

Read Ephesians 4:11-16. Paul is telling us about the importance of being built up in our knowledge of Christ so that we won't be blown here and there by every wind of doctrine.

Instead we will grow strong in Christ, completing the works that God has for us to do.

Knowing God's Word allows us to recognize truth and gives us purpose and the courage to follow Jesus Christ. Without the belt of truth, believers hesitate to follow Christ and wander around following anything that sounds good. This is the reason that Satan will do almost anything to keep us from claiming and wearing the belt of truth.

Dress Check:

Did you recognize a need for the Word of God in your life if you are going to confidently follow God? _absolutely_

Are you searching the Scriptures daily to get to know the truth of God? _✓_

Are you seeking to know the mind of Christ as you make decisions throughout your day? ___

Did you recognize a need to tighten the spiritual belt of truth in your life? ___

Write a prayer to God, recognizing your need for His truth in your life every day. _Lord keep me in Your truth. Let Your Word be a sure, strong foundation in my life._

Lesson 3

Have You Misplaced Your Belt?

For I am jealous over you with a godly jealousy, because I have promised you in marriage to one husband—to present a pure virgin to Christ. ³ But I fear that, as the serpent deceived Eve by his cunning, your minds may be seduced from a complete and pure devotion to Christ.
II Corinthians 11:2-3

The Liar

Look up John 8: 42-47. Jesus is rebuking the Jews in the temple, but I want you to pay special note to the description that Jesus gives of the devil. What is not found in the devil? _the truth_
What is his native language? _he speaks lies_
What is he the father of? _he is the father of lies_

Satan doesn't want us know the truth. The truth, according to John 8:32, will set us free. If we don't know the truth, we are vulnerable to the lies that the devil would tell us. What is the Apostle Paul's fear in II Corinthians 11:2-3? _Our minds become corrupted from the simplicity that is in Christ._

Paul was afraid that Christian believers would be deceived by the cunning of the devil. The devil will mix truth and lie hoping to deceive the unwary. Remember that he often comes disguised as an angel of light. He often wears camouflage. We need to know the truth so we can recognize the lies.

Have you heard the story of the new bank employee being instructed to be cautious of counterfeit money? The novice bank teller wanted to know everything about the counterfeit bills. What do they look like? Which colors were different? How did they feel etc.? The much wiser boss told her that instead of studying all the variations of the counterfeit bills, she should study and know the real bills. With the knowledge of the true bills, she would be able to recognize a fake bill when she saw it. You see, we too are much more likely to recognize error, the lies of the devil, after we have spent time in the Word of God, studying the truth.

The devil wants to keep us from the truth. He is determined to keep Christians from spending time in the Word. One of the most widespread and accepted lies that he tells is "You don't have time to read the Bible." Sometimes the enemy comes disguised as an angel of light and fills your life with so many "good things" to do that you neglect God's Word.

I ask you to evaluate your life and see if you have been deceived. I remember reading a statement many years ago that said "Busyness in the King's business is no excuse for ignoring the King." We need to be in the Word of God, to know the truth of God, in order to move ahead for the kingdom of God.

We live in a world that is full of the devil's lies, and it is often difficult to discern the truth. Our world certainly doesn't promote the truth of God's word, and if we don't purpose to spend time studying it, eventually the repeated lies that we hear end up, at least in part, as what we believe.

The Bride of Christ - Deceived

Satan can deceive us if we don't know the truth. In Revelation 3:17, we read a statement that the Church, the Bride of Jesus, will declare about herself: **17 Because you say, 'I'm rich; I have become wealthy and need nothing,'** This proud, self-sufficient declaration came from a deceived Bride. Jesus responded to her announcement by saying, **and you don't know that you are wretched, pitiful, poor, blind, and naked.** The Truth spoke, and He said "the truth is this; you are wretched, pitiful, poor, blind and naked." She had been deceived.

The word *blind* in this verse is the Greek word *tuphloo* meaning to make blind.[5] The root of that word speaks of being blinded by smoke or a state of high-mindedness.[6] The idea is that

---

[5] Strong, James, *A Concise Dictionary of the Words in the Greek Testament* (Nashville, TN: Abingdon Press, 1890) #5186, page 73

[6] Ibid, #5185 & 5187, page 73

something has clouded clear vision. Spiritually speaking, we live in a world that's filled with smoky lies of the devil. He's a deceiver and he's trying to confuse and blind as many people as possible to the truth of God.

In Revelation 3:18, Jesus offers his Bride <u>eye salve</u> for her eyes that she might see. I believe that <u>the eye salve is the Word of God</u>. When we know the truth of God's Word and apply it to our lives, we can see clearly the way to take. We will have discernment in the midst of all the smoky lies around us. We need the truth of God's Word daily in order that we might not be blinded.

I lived in the heart of New York's Adirondack Mountains for many years, and the first summer we cleared land and built our home, we had many visitors. Some visitors we enjoyed; others were not quite so welcome. The unwelcome type came in the form of long, slimy, hissing creatures. Apparently, the snakes hadn't gotten the notification that new residents had moved in. The snakes were on our sidewalk, on our steps, in the middle of the lawn etc. You can probably guess that I don't like snakes. I am not opposed to them living in the woods somewhere but I am not interested in them living in my yard.

I hesitate to tell this story knowing that some of you may be snake lovers. All I can say is that you can trust me when I say that I've heard all the lectures about the benefits of snakes . . . my sister had **pet** snakes! Unlike my sister, I hate snakes and wanted to eliminate their presence from my lawn.

My plan involved carrying a garden hoe in my hand, actually approaching the snake and swinging the hoe in such a manner that the snake would meet a quick demise. The first time I attempted this, I was terrified. I am 5'5" and I knew that I out-weighed the snake by a **significant** amount, yet I was afraid that the snake was going to attack, hurt, or possibly kill me. I got to within about 15 feet of the snake and wished that my hoe would somehow grow. Never taking my eyes off the snake, I cautiously advanced a few more feet until my hoe would reach and I took my first swing. I closed my eyes, screamed, and ran back 15 feet to make sure I was safe. Since that day, I have killed many snakes. While it's still not an enjoyable task, I don't run and scream anymore. I approach the snake with confidence that I will overcome it. Why? What made the difference? I stopped believing that the snake was more powerful than I. It was only after the truth that **I** had the advantage over the snake began to sink in, that the fear left me. I was bigger and more powerful than the snake, but as long as I believed that **it** had the power, I was afraid and nearly paralyzed to do anything about its presence.

Now why do I take the time to tell you about the snakes in my yard? Because the enemy is like the snake; he is **defeatable** when we believe the truth. He does not want you to discover that the Spirit of God living within you protects you from his lies because he would then lose his control over you. Ladies, get to know the truth of God, believe God, and walk with courage and confidence following the direction of God's Word. Write out Psalm 25:4-5. *Show me Your ways, O LORD; teach me Your paths. 5 Lead me* *in Your truth and teach me, For You are the God of my salvation; On You I wait all day.*

We need to be prepared for the daily spiritual battles that we face. Buckle your belt of truth in place. This doesn't mean that we have to know the entire Bible by heart, but it does mean we need to be in the Word of God enough so we can recognize lies when we hear them. When we recognize the lies, we can search the Bible for the truth and follow truth.

Psalm 119:105 Your word is a lamp for my feet and a light on my path.

 **Dress Check**:

Can you identify any of the enemy's lies that have kept you from moving ahead for God? If so, write them out here. _____

Can you find the truth of God in Scripture that exposes the lies? _____

How will you allow the truth of God's Word to free you from the power of those lies? *Your Word have I hid in my heart, that I might not sin against You - Ps 119:11*

Write a short prayer expressing your thanksgiving to God for His provision of truth to guide our every step. *Lord than You for keeping me in Your truth. Guide my every step so that I will not stumble*

Lesson 4

Warfare with the Belt

No weapon formed against you will succeed, and you will refute any accusation raised against you in court. This is the heritage of the LORD's servants, and their righteousness is from Me." This is the LORD's declaration. Isaiah 54:17

In the Old Testament, there are many examples of warfare in the history of the children of Israel. The battles came for various reasons. Sometimes because of their disobedience, God would permit an enemy nation to invade their land to humble His people and remind them that they needed Him. Other times they would engage in battle because God instructed His children to move forward and claim new land. In those situations the children of God faced battles because they were obedient.

We can face spiritual battles for the same reasons. Our disobedience can bring God's loving hand of discipline on our lives, and we will need to make a choice to humble our hearts and return to God or continue headstrong in our own direction. If we choose our way, we experience repeated defeats. There are also times in our lives when God is leading us in a new direction or expanding our area of ministry, and we may encounter tests or battles along the way.

Hard times force us to face our faith head-on. Will we choose to believe God in the middle of the hard circumstance, or will we believe the lies the enemy is whispering in our ear? When we choose to believe God and follow Him, we can be sure that we will experience a spiritual victory.

II Corinthians 2: 14 (NIV) But thanks be to God, who _always_ **leads us in triumphal procession in Christ . . .**

When the enemy notices that we are steadfastly following God, he begins a desperate battle against us, hoping to discourage us. He knows that he cannot prevail against the will of God, so his only hope is that he can cause us to doubt God's Word. If we begin to doubt God's Word, we become an easy target for his lies. There's a battle for the control of your mind. Will you choose to believe the truth of God's Word, or will you accept the lies of the enemy?

I Peter 1:13 Therefore, _Therefore, gird up the loins of your mind, be sober, rest your hope fully_ **with your minds ready for action, be serious and set your hope completely on the grace to be brought to you at the revelation of Jesus Christ.** _upon the grace that is to be brought to you at the revelation of Jesus Christ_

We are going to consider Nehemiah today in our study, but before we begin our study in Nehemiah, chapter two, let me review some events that have led up to this time.

Because of Judah's continuous disobedience to God, God allowed the Israelites to be taken captive by the Babylonians. They were slaves for 70 years until they humbled their hearts and cried to God. God's kind hand moved on behalf of His people, and the nation of Babylon was conquered by the Medes and Persians. This new ruling government was sympathetic to the plight of the captives and allowed a remnant of people to return to Jerusalem. Over the next seventy-plus years, several groups of people were permitted to return to Jerusalem. Some would come to rebuild the temple, others to bring spiritual revival, and, in the case of Nehemiah, to rebuild a wall.

In chapter one, Nehemiah received word from his brother that Jerusalem was disgraced because the wall that protected the city from attack was in complete disrepair. This saddened Nehemiah, and for four months he prayed about this matter. One day as Nehemiah served King Artaxerxes, the King asked what troubled him. Nehemiah prayed quickly and then asked the King for permission and provisions to return to his homeland to head up the mission of rebuilding the ruined wall. Because God's gracious hand was upon this task, the King willingly gave permission for Nehemiah to return and provided him with all the necessary provisions.

Dressed for the Business at Hand

Read Nehemiah 2:11-18. Who put this burden upon Nehemiah's heart (vs.12)? _God had put it in his heart what to do at Jerusalem_

Whose hand was upon Nehemiah (vs. 18)? _the hand of the Lord_

As Nehemiah surveyed the current condition of the wall, what emotions do you think that he felt? _distress he was in_

The wall that had been built to protect the holy city of Jerusalem laid in disrepair, broken and burned. As the people returned to the land, they allowed the peace of the moment to lull them into a false sense of security and they grew accustomed to living without the protection of the wall. But without the wall the people were dangerously vulnerable to attacks by enemies. In Nehemiah 2:17, Nehemiah rallied the people together and charged them with their responsibility and the need to rebuild the wall. Nehemiah wanted the people to recognize the urgency and need for protection and then be motived to do something about it.

In a spiritual analogy, the truth of God's Word provides our minds with the same type of security that a fortified wall provides a city. When the Word of God is girding up our minds, the lies of the enemy have little effect on us. The lies are exposed and repelled. But if the Word of God is not protecting our minds, we have given the enemy the upper-hand in spiritual warfare.

II Timothy 3:16-17 All _Scripture_ [given by inspiration of God] **is inspired by God and is profitable for** _doctrine_, for _reproof_, for _correction_, for _instruction_ in _righteousness_, **so that the man of God may be complete** [thoroughly], **equipped for every good work.**

Has the wall of truth, God's Word, which protects your mind, been neglected and fallen into disrepair? Have you been lulled into a false sense of security? Satan will do everything he can to keep you from knowing God's truth and living it out because he is powerless to deceive you when you have the fortified wall of God's truth surrounding your mind.

In Nehemiah 2:18, how did the people respond when challenged to rebuild the wall? _Let us rise up and rebuild._ Their ready response should be an example to us. _they set their hands to do this good work_

Nehemiah 2:19 introduces us to Tobiah, Sanballet, and Geshem. Satan used these three men to try to stop the rebuilding work. Over the next 52 days as God's people worked, they faced constant pressure, ridicule, and discouragement. The enemies attempted to fill the people with doubt about whether God had really asked them to rebuild the wall and whether God would really be there to protect them. Isn't that just like Satan? His first attack against man in the Garden of Eden was to cause Adam and Eve to doubt God's word.

Identify some of the accusations and questions that the enemies hurled against the workers as

The Belt of Truth | Week 1

they worked to rebuild the wall in Nehemiah 2:19 and Nehemiah 4:1-3? _____

"Will you rebel against the king?" 2:19

They were furious and very indignant and mocked the Jews. in the form of conspiracy.

In each situation how did the people respond (Nehemiah 2:20; 4:4-6)?
( ) They believed the enemy and gave up
(✓) They prayed to God and worked with all their hearts.

Throughout the 52 two days it took to rebuild the wall, the enemies were persistent and relentless in trying to keep the wall from being rebuilt. Why do you think this was the case?

They did not want the temple to be rebuilt, Jerusalem to be reconstructed and rebuilt.

According to Nehemiah 6:15-16, who received the glory for the completed wall? __God__

What resulted among the surrounding nations? the return to the city of their inheritance - Resettled by the people and priests

Ladies the <u>truth of God will always stand between us and the enemy</u>. The truth of God's Word assures us that we are following the only One who is true. It's only when the enemy causes us to doubt God's Word that he gains any ground against us.

Let's read about one of the last attempts to keep Nehemiah from completing the wall around the city in Nehemiah 6:5-9. Read these verses and record in your own words Nehemiah's response to the letter and his prayer to God.

The content of the letter was invented in their hearts hoping that their hands will be weakened and the work will not be done. Nehemiah prayed to strenghten his hands.

Can you pray that with me today? Lord, we want to know the truth of your Word, and we need it to <u>strengthen us to do the work that you have given us to do</u>. May we not be weakened by the lies that the enemy tells us. For your Glory, we ask this. Amen.

Dress Check:

Have you grown accustomed to living without God's Word protecting your mind?
_____
_____

Has your thinking become polluted by the enemy's lies of "anything goes" and "there aren't any absolutes"?

As you evaluate the current state of the wall of truth protecting your mind, is there need for repair work? If so, write God a prayer asking Him to strengthen your hands as you fortify your mind with the truth of His Word. *Lord, strengthen my hands and my mind with the truth of Your Word — daily. Protect me from the lies of the enemy. Give me courage to continue to do Your will for my life.*

Lesson 5

The Belt in Place

...and whenever you turn to the right or to the left, your ears will hear this command behind you: "This is the way. Walk in it." Isaiah 30:21

God appointed works for us to do for Him before we were born, and that includes being Christ's representatives to a lost and dying world (Eph.2:10, II Cor. 5:20). The challenge is how to be effective in the doing this.

Max Lucado has written a children's picture book entitled *With You All the Way*. In this tale about a medieval kingdom, three young knights are asked by a prince to travel to the king's castle. The first knight to arrive at the castle would win the hand of the princess. The journey would be difficult as each knight would be required to travel through the foreboding, dark, and confusing Hemlock Forest. The king would help guide the knights through the forest by playing a beautiful melody on his flute three times a day from the castle. If the knights listened carefully for this melody, they would be led safely through the forest to the castle. The prince then demonstrated the king's specific melody to each of the knights. The knights listened to the melody and prepared to journey through the forest, but just before they left, they were offered the opportunity to choose a traveling companion.

Within a few days, the waiting king spotted two men stumbling out of the forest. The king immediately sent servants to meet the knight and lead him to a room where he could clean up and prepare himself for the banquet that the king had prepared in his honor. At the banquet, the king asked the knight what had been the secret of his safe travel through the forest. The knight responded that the key to his success had been the traveling companion he had chosen. He had chosen the king's son, the prince himself, because the prince knew the melody of the king's flute in his heart. The knight explained that he knew as he traveled through the forest he would hear many imitations of the melody and to guarantee that he only followed the king's melody, he had asked the prince to travel with him. The prince would enable him to discern the king's melody from all the imitations. By choosing the prince as his traveling companion, the king and his music had been with the knight all the way.

What a great allegory! It has a solid lesson for us today. We need God's help to live safely in this wicked world. Temptation and sin sit at our doorstep everyday. The opportunities for us to get off track and follow something other than God are countless. Yet God has asked us to live holy and to bring the good news of salvation to others. How can we ever be successful in this endeavor? How will we avoid getting lost ourselves? How will we be able to quiet the noises of the world around us, so we will hear the voice of God leading us?

The answers to these questions are all found in how you answer this question: How close are you walking to the "flute player"? If you are attempting to walk through this sinful world using your own judgment as your compass, you are in grave danger of sin's grasp. The only safe and sure way to travel through this world is with the voice of God speaking truth in your ear every day.

As Paul neared the end of his life's journey, he wrote a letter to Timothy who he loved like a son. In this letter Paul explained how important it was to know the truth of God's Word so that Timothy could live his life in a way that was pleasing to God.

We need to know the truth

Write out II Timothy 2:15. _____
_____

Paul told Timothy to "Be diligent." In the KJV this phrase is translated "study." This meant that Timothy was to engage himself in the work of getting to know God's Word. As Timothy studied God's Word, the knowledge that he gained would allow Timothy to stand unashamed before God.

We make choices every day, and these choices are often between God's way or our own way. As we study and know the Word of God, decisions in life become easier because we have the compass of God's truth to guide us.

Read John 14:15-31.

Jesus is also speaking to His disciples one last time and He is sharing some crucial last minute warnings. In verses 15, 21, 23, 24; Jesus makes references to the importance of obeying what? _____

He even said the degree in which you follow His commands indicates how much you love Him. It was important for the disciples of Jesus to know His commands if they were going to be obedient to them.

Jesus also promises in verses 16, 17, 18, 25, 26 that He will not leave his followers as orphans but that He would send whom?_____

What is the title that Jesus gives Him in verse 17? _____
We have been given the Bible, God's words to us, and we have been given the indwelling Spirit of God to help us understand God's truth.

The Truth needs to know us

Paul informs Timothy in chapter 3, that perilous times will come. Times in which men will claim to believe God, but their lifestyles will not agree with their words. Paul warns Timothy to hold fast to the Scriptures that he has learned from an infant, for in them he will find the wisdom to live.

   Write out II Timothy 3:16-17. _____
_____

These verses tell us that all Scripture is God-breathed. The very breath of God has spoken these words to us. We can know for certain that they are absolute truth.

As we face the myriad of decisions that must be made each day, we wish that God would just tell us what to do. My friend, hear me as I say, God **has** spoken to you and He has recorded his words upon paper that you might know the way to take. This book that we call 'the Bible' is a collection of God's words to us. His words are alive and they apply to your life today. If you are feeling far from God and unsure of the way to take, open His book and bring it close to you, let your eyes fall upon His words, and seek His way.

Write out the specific functions, listed in verse 16, that God's Word will have in our lives. You may find it helpful to look at each word in the dictionary to fully understand the role each word has in your life.
   1._____
   2._____
   3._____
   4._____

We need to let God's Word penetrate our hearts and minds. We need to be open and honest with God about the way we are thinking and behaving. He already knows it anyway. But for His Word to change these areas in our lives, we need to acknowledge our need of change, being honest with Him so His Word can do its transforming work in us.

As each of these functions of the Word are applied in our lives, the result will be **[17] so that the man of God may be complete, equipped for every good work. II Timothy 3:17**

The truth was to be made known

Read II Timothy 4:1-7.

What was motivating Paul to write to Timothy (vs. 1)? _____
_____

What was the specific charge that Paul gave to Timothy (vs. 2)? _____
_____

Because of the presence of God, the presence of Jesus, and in view of the coming kingdom, Paul felt compelled to order Timothy to be prepared to "preach the Word." The Word of God is the only thing that will change the hearts of mankind. Timothy was to be ready to share this Word with patience to all who would hear it.

Paul warned Timothy that there would come a time when men would not want to hear the truth. Instead they would prefer to listen to teachers who would tell them things they wanted to hear. They would abandon truth and begin to believe lies. This sounds very much like our present world. Our world embraces the philosophy that there is no absolute truth, and by accepting this lie, they believe they can forge their own paths to the Kingdom of God. Unfortunately for them, Jesus said in **John 14:6 Jesus told him, "I am the way, the truth, and the life. No one comes to the Father except through Me.**

My paraphrase of Paul talking to Timothy in this passage is, "Timothy, you live in this world that is filled with lies, but don't be deceived by them. You keep doing the works I have called you to do."

Paul had fought a good fight; he had finished the course that God had laid out for him. Paul calls this course in verse 7 a "race." He had not meandered through life, hesitatingly wondering what to do or where to go next. He followed hard after God with his ear tuned to truth; he had run the race and completed the works that God had ordained for him to do. Some of Paul's last words to Timothy: **The Lord will rescue me from every evil work and will bring me safely into His heavenly kingdom. To Him be the glory forever and ever! Amen. II Timothy 4:18**

Dressed with the belt of truth, the knowledge of the precious Word of God, and with the Spirit of God in you to guide you into all truth, you don't need to fear entering spiritual battles. When life's realities press on you from all sides, you won't lose your head and wander aimlessly following whatever seems best at the moment. You will know the Word, the Word will know you, and you will respond to those situations with your mind girded up with the truth of God's Word. You will be able to confidently follow Jesus through it all. Tuck in your cloak and make haste. Victory is yours for the claiming!

Dress Check:

As you evaluate your life today, are you alone in that dark perilous forest, trying to hear the sound of the flute? _____

How close is the flute player to you? _____

If you have realized that you have been trying to navigate through life without the guidance of God's Word in your life every day, what will you do to change the situation? _____
_____

Once you begin to know the Word and your path becomes clearer each day, you need to allow the Word to know you. How will your prayer life change as you invite the Word of God to teach, rebuke, correct, and train you? _____
_____

Are you looking for ways to make the Word of God known to others? If so, write out the ways you are doing this. _____

If not, ask God to make known to you people that He would have you "preach the Word" to.
_____
_____

Write out Psalm 119:165. _____
_____
_____

Are you **running** your race for Jesus? If not, gird up your loins, tighten your belt, and begin to make haste!

The Belt Modeled by the Savior

A careful and detailed study of the book of Ephesians will reveal to us that the Apostle Paul did not randomly place a few verses at the end of his letter to the people of Ephesus about a spiritual suit of armor we should wear. Paul introduced us to the various truths of the armor as he wrote the book. The value of the knowledge of Christ is so that we are not like little children easily tossed by every wind of doctrine (Ephesians 4:13-14). We are to mature in our knowledge and understanding of Christ as that will be our anchor in whatever storm of life we encounter.

Paul begins his description of our spiritual armor with the belt of truth because it is essential that this belt of truth be in place before any of the other pieces of armor can be effective. If you are going into battle, the most basic and essential piece of knowledge is which side you are on. We have to know who we are following!

A soldier going to battle in Old Testament days would tuck his long gown into his belt creating a type of pant in order to step with confidence onto the battle field. Without the belt, one would trip on the long garment as he moved forward with urgency, rendering him ineffective in a battle.

The belt of truth is our knowledge of Christ and His word. Knowing God's Word allows us to know with certainty who we are following each day (Psalm 119:105). Everything that we experience in a day we filter through the truth of Christ and His Word to determine our decisions and reactions.

Satan will try to keep us from completing the works that God has planned for us to do. He does not want any lives to be changed by God so he will try to distract us from knowing Christ. He would love to convince you that reading God's Word is unnecessary. But if we do not gird our minds with the Word of God, we will be ineffective in completing the works that God has for us to do. If we don't know Jesus, it will be very hard for us to reveal Him to the world. If we are going to walk confidently following Jesus, we simply must know the Word of God.

In Ephesians, chapter 6, we are introduced to five pieces of defensive armor and one piece of offensive weaponry. The Word of God is the only piece that has application both offensively and defensively. This week we have examined the defensive protection that the Word of God offers.

As we consider our study on the belt of truth, let's take a look at a personal attack that Satan made against Jesus and see how Jesus used God's Word to protect Himself from the lies Satan was telling Him.

Read Luke 4:1-13.

Dressed for the Business at Hand

The first point of protection that the belt of truth offers is that it exposes the lies of the enemy.

Jesus' baptism was a declaration that He was moving into His public ministry of revealing God to people by completing the works that God had planned for Him. Immediately after His baptism, the Spirit of God led Jesus into the wilderness for 40 days. This would be a time of testing for Jesus.

> *Satan didn't know God's plan for Jesus. (Imagine his surprise on resurrection morning.) He doesn't know God's plan for your life either. Take comfort in that and press on following Jesus!*

Satan was not long in making his appearance; his goal was to cause Jesus to doubt God's provision, His plan, and His protection. The enemy knew that if Jesus began to doubt God, then Jesus might be tempted to stop following God, and by default, not complete the works that God had planned for Him. Satan didn't know what God's plan was for Jesus; he just knew that he wanted to disrupt and distract Jesus from completing those works.

The language in the gospel of Luke suggests that the devil tempted Him for 40 days which illustrates the persistence of the enemy. Each time the enemy tempted Jesus, he cast doubt on

* God's ability to meet Jesus' needs,
* The plan that God had for Him,
* God's power to protect Him.

Jesus responded each time with Scripture that clearly exposed Satan's lies.

The enemy's attacks will be personal against each of us. He is familiar with our vulnerabilities and will exploit us in those areas. His goal is to confuse us and cause us to doubt God so that we will choose our own way and not follow God, completing the works that He has planned for us. If the enemy is successful in convincing us to make our own way, we will be ensnared to do his will (II Timothy 2:24-26).

Romans 12:2 tells us if we want to know God's will, we need to have our minds renewed so that our way of thinking is changed. How do we do that? As we study God's Word, the truth of God's Word washes over our minds, and we are no longer confused by lies.

Psalms 119:11 I have treasured Your word in my heart so that I may not sin against You.

The belt of truth strengthens us to resist the enemy.

Jesus was emotionally and physically weakened as a result of His forty-day fast. If He had relied on His human strength to resist the devil, He would have succumbed to the tenacity of the devil. Jesus knew that God's Word had divine power and would do the supernatural work of resisting the devil.

Jesus quoted Scripture in response to each of the temptations, and verse 13 tells us that the devil left Him. God's Word caused the devil to flee. James 4:7 says, **Therefore, submit to God.**

The Belt of Truth

But resist the Devil, and he will flee from you. When we recognize and submit to the authority of God and His Word, we are able to resist the devil's lies, and the divine power of God causes the devil to flee.

Luke tells us that the devil left him until an opportune time to return. The devil will keep coming and coming and coming. He is determined to destroy the work that God is completing in us and through us. We need to be ever vigilant because he will lie to us when he thinks we are most vulnerable (I Peter 5:8). We don't need to fear his appearance because God's Word gives us divine power to resist him when he comes.

II Corinthians 10:3-5 For though we live in the body, we do not wage war in an unspiritual way, ⁴ since the weapons of our warfare are not worldly, but are powerful through God for the demolition of strongholds. We demolish arguments ⁵ and every high-minded thing that is raised up against the knowledge of God, taking every thought captive to obey Christ.

> *The importance of developing a deep love for the Word of God and for the voice of the One who speaks to us as we study is that it will keep us from being deceived and following after the enemy.*

In our own strength we have no power against the evil forces of this world, but God's Word tells us that divine power is available.

According to Ephesians, chapter 6, we can face the enemy and still be standing if we have armed ourselves with the spiritual protection that God offers to us. The first line of defense we have against the enemy is the truth; it exposes his lies and strengthens us to resist the lies.

The belt of truth will keep us from following the enemy.

As we spend time getting to know God's Word, we are also developing a relationship with God Himself. One of my favorite texts is found in John, chapter 10. In this passage Jesus describes Himself as our Shepherd.

The Good Shepherd always has the best interest of His sheep in mind. Verses 2-4 are especially precious to me: **The one who enters by the door is the shepherd of the sheep. ³ The doorkeeper opens it for him, and the sheep hear his voice. He calls his own sheep by name and leads them out. ⁴ When he has brought all his own outside, he goes ahead of them. The sheep follow him because they recognize his voice.**

The relationship depicted here is one of great familiarity and intimacy. The Shepherd knows each sheep by name. He calls them out of the sheepfold one by one and then He leads them with His voice. This is a relationship that has been cultivated and developed over time. The sheep have learned to trust their Shepherd explicitly and are willing to follow Him wherever He leads.

It is verse 5, however, that is especially pertinent to our topic today: **They will never follow a stranger; instead they will run away from him, because they don't recognize the voice of strangers.**

Dressed for the Business at Hand

The importance of developing a deep love for the Word of God and for the voice of the One who speaks to us is that it will keep us from being deceived and following the enemy.

The knowledge of the Word of God protected Jesus from following the enemy. He had the discernment to listen for and to follow only the voice of God in His life.

John 14:30-31 I will not talk with you much longer, because the ruler of the world is coming. He has no power over Me. ³¹ On the contrary, I am going away so that the world may know that I love the Father. Just as the Father commanded Me, so I do. The love relationship Jesus had with the Father and His love of His Father's words protected Jesus from following a stranger's voice.

Are there certain areas of sin in your life that you struggle with? Do you have areas of weakness that seem to get you every time? Has the battle against certain sins gone on for years? Until you choose to resist the devil and the lies he is telling you with the Word of God, he will continue to attack and defeat you in those same areas. We become slaves to whatever we allow to master us (Romans 6:16-18).

Through the years I have written on spiral-bound index cards Scripture that reinforces the truth of God in areas that I am struggling in. I don't want to believe the lies of the enemy. I want to know God's heart on the matter.

These cards are convenient and can be carried with you in your purse or coat pocket and can be referred whenever you sense the lies of the enemy being whispered in your ear. I would encourage you to participate in this method of renewing your mind. As you memorize these verses, you will be renewing your mind, strengthening your wall, listening to the flute player, and girding up your mind. Then you will know God's good and perfect will for your life.

Listen, my son. Accept my words, and you will live many years. ¹¹ I am teaching you the way of wisdom; I am guiding you on straight paths. ¹² When you walk, your steps will not be hindered; when you run, you will not stumble. Proverbs 4:10-12

*If you have children you may wish to read the lesson on the belt of truth in *The Armored Baton* (page 149).

Week 2
The Breastplate of Righteousness

Day 1: The Breastplate Made Available

Day 2: The Breastplate in Place

Day 3: A Missing Breastplate

Day 4: The Sufficiency of the Breastplate

Day 5: The Sufficiency of the Breastplate (Part 2)

Lesson 1

The Breastplate Made Available

All of us have become like something unclean, and all our righteous acts are like a polluted garment; all of us wither like a leaf, and our iniquities carry us away like the wind. Isaiah 64:6

I trust as you completed your study on the belt of truth, you examined your life for its presence. If you discovered your mind had not been protected by the truth of God's Word, then I pray that you have the belt of truth firmly in place now. If the belt of truth was already in its proper place protecting your mind, then I hope your study highlighted its value. Once our belts are secure and our minds girded up, we are ready to move ahead with confidence to complete the works God has ordained for us to do.

I believe the list of spiritual armaments in Ephesians, chapter six are given to us in the order in which we are to put them on. The belt was the first article that we needed to put on because this piece guarantees that every step we take is placed into the footprint of the True One who is leading us. Our knowledge of the truth will prevent us from being deceived into following the enemy.

The second piece of armor that we are to firmly fasten to our bodies is the breastplate of righteousness. This piece is next on the list because it ensures that our hearts agree with what our minds know to be truth. We can have a head-knowledge of the truth of God and still pursue love relationships with idols. The breastplate of righteousness protects our hearts from the pursuit of other loves.

Let's begin this week's study with a few vocabulary words.

In the Hebrew language two distinct words are translated into English as *breastplate*. The first word is *choshen*; it means something sparkly like a gem or a pocket containing something rich, like gems.[1] This word always refers to the breastplate on the High Priest.

The other Hebrew word translated *breastplate* in the English Bible is *shiryonah*, and it means a corslet (as if twisted). This word is sometimes translated *breastplate* and other times, *coat of mail, habergeon,* or *harness.*[2]

Because those words were unfamiliar to me, I used my dictionary to understand them better.

---

[1] Strong, James, *A Concise Dictionary of the Words in the Hebrew Bible* (Nashville, TN: Abingdon Press, 1890) #2833, page 44

[2] Ibid, #8302, page 121

Webster defined the words like this:
Corslet: a piece of armor for the trunk, close fitting and often laced
Coat of mail: armor made of metal links or plates
Habergeon: a medieval jacket
Harness: a piece that goes around a horse's chest, gear and equipment

As you think about the Hebrew word *shiryonah*, describe in one or two sentences what you picture a breastplate to be like. *a protecting armor which protects the heart area — protecting the heart from arrows*

One thing I noticed was it was a tight-fitting piece of armor. This piece of armor is not going to be easily dislodged. I pictured Scarlett O'Hare from *Gone with the Wind* having her corset tied on. When a corset was tied in place, it would not be easy to take off. I also noted that it was made of durable material to be effective as a protective covering. The breastplate's basic purpose was to protect the life of the wearer.

This Hebrew word *shiryonah* is only used a few times in the Old Testament, but it is always used to describe the covering of an active soldier. This word would never be used to describe a piece of civilian clothing. This piece of armor was only worn by those actively engaged in warfare.

As I researched the word *breastplate*, I came across a fabulous passage in the book of Isaiah. Read Isaiah, chapter 59. If you have a commentary, you may find it helpful to read a detailed explanation of this passage. We will do a brief overview of the chapter today.

Write out verse one. *Behold, the LORD's hand is not shortened that it cannot save, nor His ear heavy that it cannot hear* Is. 59:1

God is looking upon His needy people and wants to save them. He is waiting to hear their cries for help. What had separated the people from God (vs. 2)? *Sin*

The next six verses in the chapter describe how deep their pit of sin was. God's people pursued a life of ungodliness, and their lives bore the fruit of their sins. Notice the results of their sins: they were deceived (vs. 3-4), unsatisfied (vs. 6), and filled with wickedness (vs.7). Their pursuit of this ungodly lifestyle brought a famine of peace (vs. 8).

Without God's peace, we will never experience satisfied souls. In verses 9-15a, we see this lack of peace propelled the people to wander around in sin like blind men unable to find their way. Their self-efforts could never deliver them from their sinful condition. Their efforts continually increased their depravity. The result was the total absence of truth. This was the condition of the hearts of God's children, and it displeased God (vs. 15).

Read verses 15b-17. God saw there was no one among His people qualified to bring justice back to His people. Verse 16 says that God was appalled that there was no one to intervene for them, and because He was appalled, God made a way of salvation for His people. What does verse 16b say God sustained His people with? _His own righteousness_

God made a way of salvation through sending His Son. God's holy righteousness would sustain Christ while He was here. He would come as a warrior to destroy the power that sin held over His people.

According to verse 17, Christ came with _righteousness_ as His _breastplate_ and the helmet of _salvation on His head_ on His head.

He came to supply righteousness and salvation for His people. Thank you Jesus!

We can never attain righteousness on our own. According to Isaiah 64:6, our righteousness is like what? _Our own righteousness are like filthy rags_

Write out Romans 3:10. _There is none righteous, no, not one_

Read Acts 4:12 and record the only way that salvation is made available to us. _through Jesus_

Write out Acts 16:31. _Believe on the Lord Jesus Christ, and you will be saved, you and your household._

I loved reading this passage as it foretold the arrival of our Savior. I marveled that He would come adorned in a breastplate of righteousness. His breastplate was firmly affixed; it would not be dislodged during His time here. Jesus was protected from the sinful pull of the world around Him because He covered His heart with the righteousness of God. What an awesome thought; God, through Christ Jesus, offers us the same covering. We are told in Ephesians 6:14 to put on the breastplate of righteousness so when the day of evil comes, we will be protected and at the battle, we will still be standing.

> **Romans 5:19 For just as through one man's disobedience ~~the~~ many were made sinners, so also through ~~the~~ one ~~m~~an's obedience ~~the~~ many will be made righteous.**

The Breastplate of Righteousness | Week 2

Dress Check:

As you read the passage in Isaiah 59, did you identify with the people's perpetual search for something to satisfy? _____

Their self-efforts led them further from the peace they were seeking. Have you ever experienced this downward spiral away from God? _____

Our Savior came to bring peace to the hearts of men. Peace was missing because people did not have the ability to live righteous lives. Jesus who came adorned in a breastplate of righteousness offers us His righteousness. Have you thanked Him for this amazing gift? If not, write a prayer to God, thanking Him that you have been rescued from the power sin had upon you and for your new robe of righteousness (Isaiah 61:10). *Lord, with joy I thank You for the garment of salvation, thank You for covering me with the robe of righteousness. So glad for my bridegroom and taking me as your bride*

Lesson 2

The Breastplate in Place

Teach me Your way, Yahweh, and I will live by Your truth. *[walk in Your truth.]* Give me an undivided mind to fear Your name. *[Unite my heart to fear]* ¹² I will praise You *[O Lord my God]*, with all my heart, Lord my God, and I will honor *[glorify]* Your name forever.
Psalms 86:11-12

I marvel when I consider that I had nothing righteous within me and that God saw fit to cover my nakedness with His own righteousness. I pray that I will never grow so accustomed to God's righteous-covering over me that I forget the dirty rags it replaced.

Yesterday, when we looked in the Old Testament at the Hebrew word for breastplate, we learned it was a close-fitting, hard, protective covering. Today we are looking at the Greek word *thorax*, which is translated breastplate in the New Testament. Having recently studied insects with my daughter in school, I recognized this word immediately because we still use the word thorax in English; it simply means chest.

This Greek word tells us that when this piece of armor is properly located, it will be covering our chest. We are not to be holding the righteousness of God in our hands. We are not to possess the righteousness of God only to lay it at our feet. The righteousness of God has been given to us by Jesus Christ as a covering and protection for our chests.

The breastplate is a defensive piece of armor and was designed to specifically cover the chest area, to protect the soldier's heart. Its ultimate purpose was to protect the heart from any foreign object that would attempt to penetrate the chest and wound the heart.

35

Dressed for the Business at Hand

Read Ephesians 6:14 and tell me where the breastplate is supposed to be. _chest area / heart_

Only as the breastplate is secured in its place can it provide the protection that we need. In a spiritual sense, why do you think we need to protect our hearts? _the heart is the central organ in our body_

What does our heart represent? _life and emotion_

Our heart is the seat of our emotions; it represents the things we love. Our motivation to accomplish, possess, or pursue things comes from our hearts. When our hearts begin to desire something, we exercise our mind and our will to pursue the object of our desire.

According to Jeremiah 17:9, what is the natural condition of our heart? _deceitful, desperately wicked, who can know it?_

Without the righteousness of God protecting our hearts, we can easily be deceived by a heart that is desperately wicked.

In Isaiah, chapter 59, God looked upon the condition of man and He saw mankind had no way to accomplish righteousness on his own. Because of this, God chose to make His righteousness available to us through the person of Jesus Christ. We have received this magnificent gift of forgiveness and righteousness and are now children of God.

The Apostle Paul is telling us in Ephesians 6 that we are involved in warfare and we need to be sure that the righteousness of God is securely in place protecting our hearts.

What do our hearts need to be protected from? Satan would love to deceive us into setting our hearts (our goals, our passions, etc.) on something other than God. He cannot change the fact that because we have accepted the gift of God's righteousness, we belong to God, but he can influence how much we love God back.

With the protection of God's righteousness on our hearts, we will wake each morning with a passionate heart toward the things of God. We will long after God and the things of God. If we are deceived into laying down our breastplate of righteousness, our hearts become vulnerable to believing the lie that we will only experience true satisfaction when we have embraced something/someone other than God.

How can we tell if our hearts have believed that lie?

Read Colossians 3:1. What are we told to set our hearts on? _the things which are above_

Would God's righteousness be a good definition of "things above"? _yes_

Look up Matthew 6:33. What are we to seek first? _the kingdom of God and His righteousness_

When you seek something, what are you doing? _You look for it / pursue it_

Read I Timothy 6:6-16. What were people seeking in verses 9-10? _riches, the love of money (lustful)_

What is the godly man told to seek? _the kingdom of God and His righteousness_

I love that the word used here is *pursue*. The Greek word is dioko, and it means "to pursue, to ensue, follow after, persecute, press forward."³ This word reminds me of the childhood game of tag. When you are in hot pursuit of the person you want to tag, your eyes never stray from them. You watch where he is going and you try to anticipate where he will go next. With every bit of effort within you, you press forward trying to lay a hand on him. You are not distracted by the flowers growing nearby. You don't notice the leaves blowing in the wind. You are not drawn away by other interests. You are single-minded in your pursuit. Spiritually speaking, we are to pursue, to make an all-out effort to grab hold of righteousness.

How much of our heart will be covered by the breastplate of righteousness if we are setting our hearts on things above and pursuing righteousness? _the whole heart_

What is Jesus' answer in Mark 12:28-30 when a young man asked Jesus what the most important commandant was? _Love the LORD your God with all your heart, soul and mind and strength_

To love the Lord with all of your heart (your longings, your desires, and your emotions), your soul, your mind, and your strength is the greatest commandment!

The evidence of the breastplate of righteousness in place will be a heart that is set on things above. When the breastplate has been securely laced and in its rightful place, protecting our hearts from the pursuit of wickedness, then our hearts will passionately seek God.

Dress Check:

Did you find evidence in your life that your breastplate of righteousness was firmly in place? _____

---

³Strong, James, *A Concise Dictionary of the Words in the Greek Testament* (Nashville, TN: Abingdon Press, 1890), #1377, page 24

Dressed for the Business at Hand

If your answer is yes, thank the Lord for this wonderful love relationship you have with Him. If you could not honestly answer yes, pray and ask God to increase your love for Him.

Lord, I want more of You and Your presence in my life. Increase my love for You. Clothe me in your righteousness

Lesson 3

A Missing Breastplate

The Lord said: Because these people approach Me with their mouths to honor Me with lip-service—yet their hearts are far from Me, and their worship consists of man-made rules learned by rote. Isaiah 29: 13

I hope as you studied yesterday and read the evidences of a heart set on things above that you recognized yourself to be in pursuit of God. Today we are going to examine a few scriptures that will point out indications of a heart not pursuing the righteousness of God. A heart that has compromised its pursuit of righteousness will begin to bear the evidences of a heart in its natural condition. I pray that if you begin to recognize yourself in this description you will draw near to God and ask Him to cleanse your heart anew.

Let's return in our Bibles to Colossians, chapter 3. We read yesterday in verse 1 that we are to set on hearts on things above. Today I want you to read verses 1-7. Pay careful attention to the list of sins outlined in verse 5; these are the sins that begin to manifest themselves in the life of a person who has not set his or her heart on the pursuit of righteousness.

List the five sins mentioned in verse 5. _____

This list of sins represents the things we will pursue if we compromise our love relationship with God and begin to seek other things to satisfy us.

The first sin mentioned is **immorality.** This word is translated from the Greek word *porneia*. This word is defined in the Greek dictionary as literally- harlotry, figuratively- idolatry.[4] Literally this word means to play the role of a harlot, a prostitute. When people play the role of

---

[4]Strong, James, *A Concise Dictionary of the Words in the Greek Testament* (Nashville, TN: Abingdon Press, 1890), #4202, page 59

a harlot or prostitute, they are sharing the intimacy of their hearts and bodies with someone to whom it does not belong. They offer the privacy of their bodies to the one who offers the highest price without realizing this adulterous lifestyle exacts a much higher price on their souls.

The philosophy of many in our world culture is actually the attitude of a prostitute—have sex with anyone whenever you feel like it. The world does not have an intimate relationship with God, and to fill that void in their lives, they pursue sexual relationships hoping to find the answer to their emptiness.

There is pressure from our culture and from our sinful hearts to pursue satisfaction from immorality; however, we are admonished in this verse to put to death (lay aside) the things that belonged to our earthly nature. We have received a new nature, God's nature, and we are not to live as we used to live.

The second part of the definition for the Greek word *porneia* included the word *idolatry*. I began to ponder the implications of a heart that refuses to set its affections upon God and God alone. I realized when I follow my earthly nature and the wickedness that it loves, I am actually turning my back on God and embracing an idol. I am choosing an imitation god over the one true God.

The second sin mentioned in this list is _____. This is the Greek word *akatharsia*, and it means uncleanness either physically or morally.[5] When my heart is not set on the pursuit of God, it will be overcome with its own wickedness. My heart will lead me along a path filled with the fruits of a desperately wicked heart (Jer. 17: 9).

The next two sins go together. The first one listed is **lust** which is the Greek word *pathos*. This particular Greek word is only used three times in the New Testament. Pathos is the soul's diseased condition out of which the various lusts spring.[6]

The second sin in this couplet is **evil desires.** This is the Greek word *epithumia*, and it means to want something you cannot have.[7] This word is used many times in the New Testament and is usually translated lust. Lust in our English language is actually a neutral word meaning to desire after something, but in this list of sins we see that a heart not set on things above will naturally desire evil things, things that dishonor the person.

---

[5] Zodhiates, Spiros, ed. *The Hebrew-Greek Key Word Study Bible* (Chattanooga, TN: AMG Publishers, 1996) #167, page 1801

[6] Ibid, # 3806, page 1862

[7] Strong, James, *A Concise Dictionary of the Words in the Hebrew Bible* (Nashville, TN: Abingdon Press, 1890) #1939, page 31

These types of desires manifest in different forms. For some people it may be the desire to indulge in sexual sins; for others it may be the desire to seek vengeance when they have been wronged or to steal something. Anytime a person indulges in an activity without exercising self-control, they are yielding to the lusts of their flesh. Can you think of other evil desires or lusts that may tempt a person?

_____
_____
_____

Without the protection of God's righteousness over our hearts, we will be led astray by the evil desires and the lusts of our hearts.

The last sin listed in this verse is greed. The definition for this Greek word *pleonexia* is an insatiable desire for things. This describes the longing that comes in a person's heart who has forsaken God and fills his or her life with lower objects.[8] Isn't that a conviction in your soul? A heart without the protection of God's righteousness will seek to fill itself with the lower objects in nature.

Summarize Romans 1:21-25. _____
_____
_____
_____

Without the covering of God's righteousness upon our hearts, we may be tempted to believe the television commercials and the magazines that say we need the newest, coolest gadget to be satisfied. The picture we saw in Isaiah 59 was of a people who constantly searched for peace but never found it. We can see this same empty search today as people look for something that will bring peace and contentment. They search but they don't find because they are not looking at the only One who can truly satisfy, Jesus. Colossians 3:5 ends by identifying greed as idolatry. Greed is forsaking God and trying to fill our hearts with the lower objects of nature.

Do you see yourself in this list of sins? Are you struggling with the pull of your heart to pursue these things? Are you afraid your need for love is not being met or will never be met? Have you found yourself pursuing the accumulation of things because you think you will find satisfaction in stuff? Is your mind occupied with how to keep your things from being stolen or lost? Do you have to rent a storage unit to store your extra stuff? What is your heart pursuing?

This passage in Colossians has instructed us to put to death the sins that grow out of a heart not

---

[8] Zodhiates, Spiros, ed. *The Hebrew-Greek Key Word Study Bible* (Chattanooga, TN: AMG Publishers, 1996) #4124, page 1867

set on things above. If the sins we examined today are present in our lives, we can be sure that we have laid aside our breastplate and the enemy has penetrated our hearts with a passion for something other than God.

Read James 4:4-10. In this passage James is speaking to believers who claim to be following God and seeking Him, yet James points out they had become friends with the world. A believer who embraces the world is called what is verse 4? _____

There are ten action verbs in James 4:7-10 that outline the remedy for restoring an intimate relationship with God. Which specific action is required of the heart in verse 8? _____

This word *purify* in the Greek means to make chaste. A heart that has strayed from a pure relationship and has committed adultery needs to be made clean again.

I want to remain pure in my relationship with Christ. I don't want to share the intimacy of my cleansed heart with the enemy. I need to make sure that I have put on the breastplate of Christ's righteousness every day. Only then will I walk purely and chastely as the beloved Bride of Christ. With His breastplate firmly affixed over my heart, I will be able to withstand the enemy's assault on my heart when he tempts to steal me away for a moment of adulterated sin.

Matthew 6:21 For where your treasure is, there your heart will be also.

Dress Check:
In the last two days, we have seen the evidences of a heart protected by the breastplate of righteousness and the evidences of a heart that has been compromised. Be silent before the Lord and ask Him to reveal the current condition of your heart.

Dressed for the Business at Hand

Lesson 4

The Sufficiency of the Breastplate
And my God will supply all your needs according to His riches in glory in Christ Jesus.
Philippians 4: 19

Have you ever looked in your closet and found nothing to wear? My husband thinks this happens all too often to me. For whatever reason, the clothes hanging in my closet come up short of my desires or expectation for them. In our town we have a nice solution called the Share Shop. It's a used clothing store run by our local church and it offers free clothes. I can take my desire for something newer or more satisfying and walk through the clothing store, until I find just the right thing that will meet my current need. The trouble with the satisfaction that comes from something new is that it never lasts. As styles change, or my weight changes, I am always looking for something new.

The protective armor that God offers to us in Ephesians is one-size fits all and its style never goes out of date. The enemy, however, would love to convince us that God's Word is outdated and can't meet our needs. He would love to persuade us that times have changed and we need to exchange the old for something new and more exciting. He prevails upon us to trade God for a more modern belief system. Sometimes we are subtly tempted to modify our faith in little ways, like believing we need God plus something else to be satisfied.

Today, my desire is that you will know the all-sufficiency of Jesus Christ in your life. As we pursue righteousness, we have many assurances in scripture that our souls will be satisfied. Because there are so many promises of this blessed contentment, it would be impossible for us to study them all in the next two days, so I have chosen to focus on the seven **I Am's** of Christ, found in the Gospel of John. As we look at these seven proclamations of Christ, we will see the total and absolute sufficiency of Christ to our souls.

#1
The first declaration is found in John 6:35. What does Jesus say that He is? _____

What is the promise given to those that come to Him? _____

As human beings, we are well aware of our need to eat to satisfy the hunger pangs that come when we fail to eat regularly. In this verse Jesus identifies Himself as the Bread of Life. He offers Himself to us as the very thing we need to satisfy our soul's hunger. We will never need to seek anyone or anything else to fill us. He is all we need. In the preceding verses of this chapter, Jesus had just fed 5,000 hungry people. This group of people had experienced a supernatural meal and they were following Jesus because they hoped he would meet their physical needs again. Jesus had met their physical needs, but more importantly, He had come to meet their spiritual need.

John 6:51 tells us that when we partake of this Bread of Life we will have what? _____

Before Jesus came, we were dead in our trespasses and sins. Sin had brought a spiritual death to man and we needed the gift of life that Jesus was bringing to us. John 1:4 tells us that Jesus came to bring life. The life that Jesus offers us is not for a day, a month, or a season, but for all eternity.

In John 6:35 Jesus said that He was the Bread of Life and all who would come to Him would never be hungry and all that believed in Him would never what? _____

John chapter 4:4-14 contains the account of Jesus meeting the Samaritan woman at the well and promising her that He could satisfy her thirst. What promise did Jesus make to those who accept the living water He offers (vs. 14)? _____

Paraphrase in two-three sentences what the Psalmist knew about being satisfied with God, in Psalm 63:1-5. *His lovingkindness is better than life.*
_____
_____

Can you think of other verses that talk about Christ satisfying our longings as the Bread of Life or as our thirst quenching water?
_____
_____
_____
_____

> **John 12:35-36** Jesus answered, "The light will be with you only a little longer. Walk while you have the light so that darkness doesn't overtake you. The one who walks in darkness doesn't know where he's going. **36** While you have the light, believe in the light so that you may become sons of light." Jesus said this, then went away and hid from them.

When we choose to pursue Christ and to love him with our whole hearts, we can be confident that He will be the Bread of Life and the spring of living water to our souls. We will not be found lacking; instead, we will be filled to overflowing.

#2

The second I AM of Christ is found in John 8:12. How does Jesus identify Himself in this verse? _____

What promise does he give to those who follow Him?
_____

Imagine yourself waking in the middle of the night during a power outage and for some unknown and bizarre reason you have to get up and start your day. Picture yourself functioning in total blackness trying to pack school lunches, make breakfast, etc. It would be a huge struggle as you tried to make sense of each article in the darkness. You would not experience peace and contentment until what happened? _____

The promise from Christ in His declaration of being the Light of the World is that He will satisfy our desire to see and understand life's true purpose. We were created in the image of God, and mankind was crowned with glory. When sin entered the world, we became dead in our trespasses and sin and we became children of darkness. With Christ as our Savior, we become children of God again and thereby children of light. Only then can we experience the true satisfaction of understanding our true purpose, to glorify God.

I have known people who, because they have never accepted the Light of the World, have been on a perpetual quest to find the right hobby, job, or relationship to bring satisfaction into their lives. They have moved from one activity to another, constantly searching. They will never find satisfaction until they look into the face of the One who promises to be our Light. Without the presence of Jesus in their lives, they grope in the blackness hoping to find something to satisfy them.

Do you have other verses that are dear to you that talk about Christ being the light in our lives? If so which ones? _____

Do you bask in the "Sonlight?" Write out Psalm 119:105. _____
_____

We have the light and life of His Spirit within us, and we have been given the lamp of His Word to light our way.

#3

Another wonderful title that Christ ascribes to Himself is found in John 10:7-10. What name do we find here? _____

What promises are given to those who enter by way of Christ (Vs. 9-10)? _____
_____
_____

Isn't that beautiful? We are given the gift of salvation, the saving of our souls from the penalty of sin. We are saved through Him, and we have the security of the sheepfold to call our own, but we are also permitted to go to the pasture where sheep find food and rest under the watchful eye of the shepherd.

These verses also mention an enemy who wants to destroy the sheep. We learn in verse five that because the sheep have been trained to follow their shepherd's voice it is unlikely they would follow a stranger's voice. I wonder if the enemy held out his hand, filled with enticing treats, if he could tempt a sheep to bury his nose into the pile of treats and walk out past the safety of the gate. The treats would provide momentary satisfaction, but that satisfaction would evaporate quickly as the hand that lured the sheep from the sheepfold withdrew the treats and returned with a sword. I pray that if my nose is ever buried into the enemy's treats that I will hear Christ's gentle voice speak my name before I ever walk past my all sufficient Gate.

#4

The next declaration of Jesus Christ ties very closely to His title of Gate. In John 10:11, Jesus calls himself _____.

Having just read the previous verses, I am glad that we are in the hands of the Good Shepherd. The Good Shepherd's intentions are always in our best interest. In verses 11-15, we read some characteristics of the Good Shepherd. List the qualities that you see. _____
_____
_____

It's the ultimate comfort to my soul to know that Jesus, the Good Shepherd, has my very best in His heart at all times. He came to bring us life at the expense of His own life. But isn't that what a good shepherd would do -- love his flock, provide for his flock, protect his flock at all costs, even the highest cost? I can rest in the sufficiency of Christ in my life when I understand this all-encompassing love toward me. It was His great love for me that caused Him to give His very life for the redemption of mine. I can trust He will continue to love me with that same degree of greatness and meet my every need.

Dress Check:

Have you experienced the fullness of life that Christ has offered to those who come to Him? _____

Do you know the joy of walking in the Light of life? _____

Are you enjoying the protection that he offers as your Gate? _____

Do you know the security of being held in those nail scarred hands? _____

Would Christ ever withhold something from us that was for our good? _____

He promised us in **John 10:10 . . . I have come so that they may have life and have it in abundance.**

Lesson 5

The Sufficiency of the Breastplate

Part 2

We will examine the last three **I AM's** of Jesus today. I pray your heart is blessed as you realize that only Jesus can satisfy our every need, and He has freely offered to do so! As we set our hearts' pursuit on God and we seek His righteousness, He meets us every time, and we won't be disappointed. I have been beguiled by the enemy many times, and when I lifted my head and looked around, I discovered I had wandered in darkness away from the safety of the fold and the tender care of the Good Shepherd. I am praying as you and I study the satisfaction that only Jesus offers that we will never again be an easy target for the enemy. May our souls be filled and satisfied with the Savior.

#5

In John 11:25 Jesus makes another I AM statement.   What title does Jesus use to describe himself? _____

This chapter in John's Gospel is one of the most moving accounts of Christ's humanity. We are allowed to be eyewitnesses to the death of one of Jesus' closest friends. Lazarus had become very sick and his sisters had sent an urgent message to Jesus asking Him to return to their village so He could heal Lazarus. Jesus purposely prolonged His coming, to display His authority over death.

Jesus' heart ached when he arrived in their village and was told that Lazarus had died. The tears He shed were not for Lazarus; Jesus knew that He had the power to breathe life back into Him. His tears represented His acute awareness of the pain in Mary and Martha's hearts. Jesus wanted to display His glory in a powerful way, and He had chosen His friends to be the tool that displayed that glory. Jesus never allows pain in our lives without the hope that His glory will be revealed. Mary and Martha's pain would last for a moment, but the glory that God would reveal lasts for eternity.

When Jesus called Lazarus to come from the tomb, Jesus demonstrated that He was life and that he had power over death. When those we love are taken away from us in death and our hearts are overwhelmed in sadness, Christ offers to satisfy our grief by bringing us the peace of eternal life. When we face the prospect of our own death or the death of a loved one, we should be comforted because Jesus is the Resurrection and the Life and we have the confidence of eternal life. Those who choose to follow the ways of the wicked one never know the true satisfaction of comfort in their times of grief.

The Breastplate of Righteousness | Week 2

#6

The sixth I AM of Christ is found in John 14:6. Write the name that Christ claims as His.
_____

This verse has three titles in one, yet all titles point in the same direction-- access to God. Before Christ's sinless life and His sacrifice on the cross, people had limited access to God. People would bring their sacrifices to the temple and offer them to God, but only the High Priest had access into the Holy Place of God. Even the High Priest was only permitted to enter the Holy Place once a year during Passover. Entering the presence of God in the Holy Place was a privilege that only a few chosen people ever had. Praise God out loud with me that He has made a Way for us to come to Him. Only when we come into His presence in the Truth of His Son do we have Life.

Read Leviticus 16:1-4. Did Aaron have permission to enter the Most Holy Place whenever He desired? _____

Why not (vs. 2)? _____

What would happen to him if he came into the Most Holy Place in an unholy manner (vs. 2)?
_____

Aaron was required to bring which two animals to the Lord first (vs. 3)? _____

They were to be slain as sacrifices for what two offerings (vs. 3)? _____

Was Aaron required to wear special clothing? _____

Before he dressed in the special clothing, he was instructed to do what to his body (vs. 4)?
_____

This passage is a clear description of the strict rules that the High Priest had to follow to prepare to be in the presence of God. Once a year, one man, who followed the guidelines exactly and brought a sacrifice to cover his sins, could safely enter the presence of God.

Jesus Christ is telling us in John 14:6 that He has become the Way, the Truth, and the Life. Celebrate with me that because of Christ's blood sacrifice, our souls have been cleansed, we have been adorned with the special garment of Christ's righteousness, and we have been granted access into God's presence with the same privilege that Christ has, access as a son-- a child of God.

Galatians 4:4-7 tells us that we have received the full rights of what? _____

Dressed for the Business at Hand

Write our Hebrews 4:16. _____
_____
_____

The longing in our hearts to know God is satisfied when we get to know 'the Way, the Truth, and the Life." There is no other way to the Father. There is no other way to have peace with God. The enemy would tell us there are many other ways to know that peace. The Bible says in **Matthew 7:13-14 Enter through the narrow gate. For the gate is wide and the road is broad that leads to destruction, and there are many who go through it. [14] How narrow is the gate and difficult the road that leads to life, and few find it**. May our hearts be satisfied in the presence of God!

#7

The seventh and final IAM of Christ is found in John 15:1. Write out this wonderful verse.
_____
_____

I am not an expert gardener by any stretch of the imagination, but I do plant a garden each year and I grow several types of vine plants. One thing that even I have noticed is if a branch breaks off the main vine, it stops growing and begins to decay. There are many reasons that a branch may be severed from the vine, but the result is always the same, death. Branches that remain attached to the vine flourish and grow. Jesus tells us that He is our vine. He will provide our sustenance for life if we stay attached to Him.

If we abide in Him, we will bear what (vs. 4-5)? _____

We develop mature fruit. Contained within that mature fruit are seeds that will guarantee another crop of fruit.

Verse six is a sad verse to me because it describes what happens to a branch when it chooses not to stay attached to the vine. The branch withers and ultimately dies. This withering and death is exactly what Satan wants. He wants us to become unsatisfied with our Vine and to cut ourselves off from its nourishment. He will provide many opportunities for us to do this, but the result is always a withering of our souls. Instead of finding a more satisfactory life, we will experience the emptiness of soul.

Verses 7-8 have often been misunderstood to be a health and wealth promise, but what promise does Christ offer to the abiding fruit? _____

If you were a fruit hanging on a vine, what types of things would you desire from the vine?
_____

The Breastplate of Righteousness | Week 2

If you lacked a particular nutrient to grow to your fullest potential and you asked the vine to send that nourishment to you, do you think the vine would supply your need? _____

What if you said to the vine, "Hey, I could really use an easy chair down here; it is a little hard sitting on the ground. And while you are at it, could you send me an umbrella? I need shelter from the hot sun!" Those requests are self-serving and are not in the best interest of the plant and its desire to produce fruit. I am certain that the vine would not answer those types of requests.

The promise in these verses is that we can ask Christ for what we need in order to grow; because as we flourish and grow, the vine itself is honored. Sometimes we don't even know the right things to ask for, but we have the assurance that if we ask and if we need them, He will give them to us.

As we remain (abide) in the true Vine, we will know the love of God and according to verse eleven we will be filled with what? _____. The text in the HCSB reads that our "joy will be complete." This means that our joy will not be lacking. Hallelujah! When we abide in the Vine, we will be satisfied with joy and we will not be led astray by the enemy who would try to convince us that true joy is found in earthly things.

This small study on the sufficiency of Christ has been such a blessing to me. It has made me aware of some vulnerable areas in which the devil might tempt me. I have clearly seen that he has nothing to offer me that will ever satisfy my heart. I know that true satisfaction will come only as I pursue the righteousness of God. I have begun to pray daily that my heart will be protected by the breastplate of righteousness. I pray that I will never be deceived into unlacing my breastplate and laying it down. My desire is that God would always look upon my heart and know that it belongs to Him with wholehearted devotion.

If we have faithfully worn the breastplate of righteousness in this life, keeping our hearts pure for the one true God, what will be waiting for us in Heaven according to II Timothy 4:7-8?

_____

That is huge motivation to me, to keep my heart chaste and pure for Him and Him alone. I want to long after God and the things of God with my whole heart.

Dress Check:

As we close our homework this week, I would like you to consider the following. Before company arrives at my house, I usually spend an entire day or most of the day, picking up, straightening, and putting things away. Then I dust, sweep, and vacuum until all signs of disorder and dirt have been removed. When I hear someone say that they cleaned their house in an hour, I figure that it really wasn't that messed up to begin with because cleaning a whole house takes time. My children are notorious for cleaning their tornado- swept rooms in about 10 minutes. When they call me to inspect their rooms, I know before I even arrive that the rooms are not clean as it would be physically impossible to have made order out of disorder in that short of time.

Ladies if it has been a while since you have examined your heart, cleaned up, picked up and put things back into their right places, it is time for you to put forth the effort. The Spirit of God has taken up permanent residence in our lives. He promises to dwell with us always and to comfort and satisfy our souls, but sometimes we forget that He desires to inhabit our **entire** hearts. We may have allowed some areas of our hearts to become cluttered and disorganized. It's even possible that we have allowed some idols to be built in the hidden rooms of our hearts. If it has been some time since you have aired out and straightened each room of your heart, take the time now to examine what is out of place. Some things will need to be thrown out, some things will need to be put away, some things will need to be dusted, and all idols will need to be broken down. When we have totally surrendered our hearts to His presence, He will truly fill our hearts, and we will experience the satisfaction that He desires to bring to us. Take time now for some spring cleaning in your heart!

A New Heart

Ephesians 4:17-24 Therefore, I say this and testify in the Lord: You should no longer walk as the Gentiles walk, in the futility of their thoughts. [18] They are darkened in their understanding, excluded from the life of God, because of the ignorance that is in them and because of the hardness of their hearts. [19] They became callous and gave themselves over to promiscuity for the practice of every kind of impurity with a desire for more and more. [20] But that is not how you learned about the Messiah, [21] assuming you heard about Him and were taught by Him, because the truth is in Jesus. [22] You took off your former way of life, the old self that is corrupted by deceitful desires; [23] you are being renewed in the spirit of your minds; [24] you put on the new self, the one created according to God's likeness in righteousness and purity of the truth.

The breastplate of righteousness, the covering of God, protects our hearts and satisfies our souls! We have been rescued from the domain of darkness and its deceitful desires. We have put on our new self, created in the likeness of God's righteousness!

In our spiritual battles, we are constantly being bombarded with messages that God isn't enough, that we need to place our hope in something else besides God. Only when our hearts are set on things above, protected by Christ's righteousness, can we steer clear of believing and following those deceitful temptations.

We have been given a new heart, one that has been purified and filled with the Spirit of God. Our heart belongs to Jesus!

What an amazing thought. The God of the universe who spoke and the worlds came into being pursued the darkened heart of man and made a way for our hearts to be made new and indwelt by Him. This is grace, amazing grace.

It almost seems ludicrous that the one who was pursued by such an amazing love would ever be tempted to turn away from the lover of his soul, but Scripture has recorded many such instances for us to learn by. I Corinthians 10:6 tells us that all that happened to Israel in the Old Testament is an example for us. And throughout the Old Testament, we are front-row witnesses to God's love story with the nation of Israel and its choice to leave God to engage in worship of false gods.

One of the predominant reasons we see this happen is fear, fear that what they have is not enough. Fear is a huge motivator. Remember in our first lesson I pointed out that the enemy tempted Jesus to doubt Gods provision, His plan, and His protection. As soon as we doubt that God is enough in any one of these areas, fear will push us towards trying to find a way to take care of ourselves. We can watch the wicked around us who seem to prosper while we struggle and, pretty soon, we doubt God's provision and begin to seek ways to prosper. This was one of the arguments that Israel had with God in Malachi. They wanted what the wicked had. They doubted God's provision.

When the Israel rejected Samuel as their judge and demanded a king to rule over them, they said they wanted to be like the surrounding nations. They doubted God's plan.

When I think of Israel doubting God's protection, I think of the multiple times that the nation of Israel embraced the idols of neighboring pagan countries. The Israelites heard their neighbors talking about serving the god of fertility or the god that protected them from snakes and scorpions or the god of the sun and they began to wonder if Yahweh, Almighty God, would also

> With their heads they were acknowledging the truth. They were willing to SAY that He was God, but their HEARTS had turned toward other gods.

protect them. In fear they began to share their worship with these other gods just in case God wasn't enough.

I can clearly see the error of their way, the doubting and fear that gave way to a divided heart. But in clearly seeing their error, I am reminded to look within my own heart for signs of division. Have I allowed doubt and fear to creep into my heart? Have I listened to the lies of the enemy enough times that I too have reached out and embraced some of our world's idols, trying to guarantee that somehow I will end up with what I need in this life. Have I shared my heart with the enemy?

One clear example of this turning of the heart is found in Jeremiah, chapter 2. Take the time to read through this chapter. I find it to be one of the saddest chapters in Scripture.

God's beloved people turn their backs on Him and look for satisfaction elsewhere, and God's displeasure in this unfaithfulness is painfully obvious.

Having once pledged her devoted love to God, the bride of God had sought after empty, worthless substitutes. God was not pleased and His utter displeasure is evident in Jeremiah 2:11-12. He exposed the paradox that the ungodly nations around them had remained faithful to their false gods despite the fact that these false gods had never been able to help them, and yet God's own beloved people forsook their God looking for something better and in turn got something worthless.

God's people had forsaken Him and pursued worthless gods. He describes their abandonment as walking away from a spring of water and choosing a hand dug cistern instead. They had walked away from the only true source of satisfaction, believing the lie that a leaking cistern would satisfy.

They would never find satisfaction, and because of that, they would search endlessly for something that would meet their need.

In verses 20-27, we see that their vain search for something to satisfy their soul-thirst would lead them to idol worship. Verse 27 is especially important in our lesson today: **They say to wood, "You are my father," and to stone, "You gave me birth." They have turned their backs to me and not their faces; yet when they are in trouble they say, Come and save us.**

With their eyes they were looking at God and acknowledging Him as their God, but their bodies had turned away so that their backs were turned to God and their hearts were facing idols. Can you picture a person's body facing in one direction with their head turned to look behind them? With their heads they were acknowledging the truth. They were willing to SAY that He was God, but their HEARTS had turned toward other gods. *idols*

Turn in your Bibles to Isaiah 29:13. This is a word from the LORD being delivered to Israel, **The Lord said: Because these people approach Me with their mouths to honor Me with lip-service— yet their hearts are far from Me, and their worship consists of man-made rules learned by rote—**

> It is not bad to have earthly possessions – but do we possess them or do they possess us?

They had head knowledge of the truth of God, but their hearts had been given over to the pursuit of other loves.

Let's read Matthew 15:8. Jesus is speaking about the Pharisees and the teachers of the law. **These people honor Me with their lips, but their heart is far from Me.** This problem of having a divided heart had traveled through the years and continues to spread in our day because it has proven to be an area that Satan uses successfully to deceive those who should know the truth.

[handwritten margin note: divided heart – God + something else]

We live in the world so that we can reveal God to people, but we are not to be side-tracked by the world, devoting ourselves to the pursuit of it.

I John 2:15-16 Do not love the world or the things that belong to the world. If anyone loves the world, love for the Father is not in him. ¹⁶ For everything that belongs to the world—the lust of the flesh, the lust of the eyes, and the pride in one's lifestyle—is not from the Father, but is from the world.

Have you ever wondered if Jesus held anything of the world dear to Him? We never hear that he brought luggage along as He traveled from town to town. There is no mention of any material possession that Jesus held dear. He knew their fleeting value. It is not wrong to have earthly possessions, but it is wrong for them to possess us.

Jesus made a way for us to have a new heart. We have been given the spring of living water, the Spirit of God, to dwell within us. The Spirit of God is our pledge, our gift of betrothal, signifying that we belong to the risen Savior Jesus Christ. One day we will be presented to our Bridegroom as His virgin bride. But we have an enemy who wants a piece of our hearts. He wants to defile us by convincing us that God is not enough and that we will only find satisfaction when we turn our hearts to other things.

There will be a battle for our hearts' devotion until Jesus comes and takes us to heaven. The enemy knows that a mind full of the truth of God's Word and a heart devoted to God is a danger to his empty, earthly kingdom, so he will surround you with all the flashing, glittering, bright-light-lifestyles of those who do not know God in an attempt to cause you to doubt that God's sufficiency!

This is a tactic that is documented many times in Scripture. We need to be aware of it. We need to be ready for it. We need to be able to resist the temptation. How can we do that? We are instructed in Ephesians, chapter 6 to wear the breastplate of righteousness. When our hearts are protected with the righteousness of God, He will occupy our thoughts, we will be seeking after Him, and our hearts will be set on things above. My heart belongs to Jesus; what about yours?

We will stand firm against the enemy when our belt of truth is protecting our minds and the breastplate of righteousness is protecting our hearts.

Dressed for the Business at Hand

Proverbs 4: 23 Guard your heart above all else, for it is the source of life.

Oh Lord, I want my heart to be Yours and Yours alone. Show me anything false that I have set up as a god in my life. I need your truth to help me recognize the devil's lies. I don't want to insult you by following the enemy and sharing my heart, which belongs to You, with him. I know that only You can satisfy my soul. As the Puritans prayed, so do I: "Lord teach me that a life that does not satisfy You, will be a life that does not satisfy me either."

*If you have children you may wish to read the lesson on the breastplate of righteousness in <u>The Armored Baton</u> (page 151).

Week 3
Feet Fitted with the Readiness that Comes from the Gospel of Peace

Day 1: Cleansed Feet

Day 2: Prepared Feet

Day 3: The Way of the Feet

Day 4: Victorious Feet

Day 5: The Most Glorious Feet

Dressed for the Business at Hand

Lesson 1

The Cleansed Feet

Because of our God's merciful compassion, the Dawn from on high will visit us
[79] to shine on those who live in darkness and the shadow of death,
to guide our feet into the way of peace. Luke 1:78-79

As I began to study the piece of armor listed in Ephesians 6:15, **feet fitted with the readiness** [having shod feet w/the preparation of the gospel of peace] **that comes from the gospel of peace (NIV)** I started by looking up the word *feet* in the Bible. My heart was blessed as I explored the various emphases placed on feet in God's precious Word.

In Ephesians we are told that our feet are fitted with the readiness that *comes from* the gospel of peace. Our feet are "fitted with readiness" only after they have received the gospel of peace. The gospel of peace is the peace we have with God based on the forgiveness that He offers us. We will investigate today what God's Word teaches us about the necessity of serving Him with cleansed feet. This is a purity we experience only after He has forgiven our sins.

Let's begin by looking up several Old Testament passages that help us understand the importance of cleansed feet. Look up these passages and record the occasions that prompted the offers to wash the person's feet.

Genesis 24:28-33 _host Laban offered water for footwashing for Abrahams servant_
Genesis 43:24-25 _Josephs servants ~~washed~~ gave water to Josephs brothers to wash their feet before Joseph would eat with them._

In each situation someone had traveled, and dirt and grime from the journey covered the guest's feet. Before a time of fellowship could be enjoyed with the host, water was offered to clean the traveler's feet, making him acceptable for fellowship in the host's home. In times past, water was routinely offered to travelers so they could freshen up. When a host offered water to a guest, he was inviting them to come and sit down and fellowship with him. When a guest accepted the water, he accepted the invitation for fellowship.

When I think of this in modern terms I picture someone traveling on a long overnight trip to visit another. Upon arrival the host offers the bathroom to freshen up. The guest may not need the water to wash his feet, but I am sure that the guest would welcome the water in order to wash his face and to brush his teeth. You can imagine that if the guest didn't brush his teeth, his opportunity for close fellowship might be lost. Cleansing is an important event before a time of close fellowship can be enjoyed.

Cleansing was instituted as a requirement for the priests serving in the Tabernacle. As you look

up these verses, write what you believe this required washing symbolized.
Exodus 30:17-21 _A requirement before worship._
Exodus 40:30-32 _Commended by the LORD before entering the meeting place._

The priests would stand before the brazen laver and wash their hands and feet before they entered the tent of meeting to serve God. According to Exodus 38:8, what was the bronze laver covered with? _mirrors_

I believe as they stood in front of that laver symbolically washing away any sin that had polluted their hands and feet, they were reminded by the mirror's reflection of their priestly garments that they had been chosen by Almighty God to serve Him. They could only enter the tabernacle to serve God once they had been cleansed.

In James 1:22-26, we are told that a man who hears the Word of God but does not do what it says, is like what (vs. 23-24)? _like a man observing his natural face in a mirror_

As we look intently into the perfect law of liberty, the Word of God, we, like the priests, can see our reflection clearly. The image that we see transfixes our minds as we understand that our filthy rags of righteousness are gone and in their place is the most glorious robe of Christ's righteousness. Without hesitation, we understand the importance of washing our hands and our feet before we enter into service and fellowship with the Father. If we walk away from our time in the Word of God, having seen our reflection, yet choosing not to freshen up, we deceive ourselves (vs. 22).

According to verse 25 the man that looks into the Word of God and does what it says will be what? _blessed in what he does_

The priests had been set apart and chosen to serve God. They believed God, and righteousness was given to them, just as righteousness has been given to us when we believe God. Yet before they could actually go into the tent of meeting where God's presence dwelt, they were required to cleanse their hands and their feet. It symbolized their need to serve in purity.

In the New Testament we are given another picture of cleansed feet. Read John 13:1-20. This passage is a very clear lesson in humility and serving others, but I would like you to pay special attention to verses 8-10. These verses record a conversation between Jesus and Peter that is especially pertinent to our lesson today.

What did Peter say to the Lord in verse 8? _You shall never wash my feet_
What was Jesus' response to Peter in verse 8? _If I do not wash you, you have no part w/ Me_
How did Peter respond to the Lord in verse 9? _Lord, not my feet only, but also my hands and my head_

Dressed for the Business at Hand

Explain what Jesus meant when He responded to Peter in verse 10.
He who is clean needs only to wash his feet, he'll be completely clean

If we have accepted Jesus' death on the cross as payment for our sins and have asked Jesus to forgive us of our sins, our souls have been cleansed by His blood (John 15:3, Acts 10:43, Acts 13:38, Eph. 1:7). We stand before the Father as children of God (Rom. 8:14, Rom. 9:26, Gal 3:26, Eph. 1:5). We have received the peace of God and that means that sin doesn't stand as an insurmountable wall between us and God anymore. Our sins have been forgiven and we have received a privilege given to sons, fellowship with the Father. We have peace with God. It is because we have experienced this peace with God that our feet have been "fitted with readiness."

We will discover in our study tomorrow that readiness means obedience. Having received the good news of God's peace, our feet have been fitted with readiness to do whatever God asks.

Today we studied the need for our feet to be cleansed. Our whole body has already been cleansed by the blood of Christ Jesus, including our feet, but as we live and function in this world we often find the dust and the filth of our sinful choices clinging to us. To prepare ourselves for close fellowship with God, we wash our hands and feet daily in the Word of God, asking Him to cleanse us from all unrighteousness. Write out 1 John 1:9. *If we confess our sins, He is faithful and just to forgive us our sins and to cleanse us from all unrighteousness.*

We do not want to allow the sin and grime of this world to build up on our spiritual feet. When a buildup of sin occurs, we discover that our fellowship with the Father is hindered and we are no longer "fitted with readiness" to do the Lord's commands. Let's keep our feet clean by bathing daily in the cleansing Word of God.

Purify me with hyssop, and I will be clean; wash me, and I will be whiter than snow. Psalm 51:7

Dress Check:

Are you allowing the mirror of God's Word to show you the areas in your life that are dust covered and in need of cleansing? _____

We would be foolish if we didn't look daily into an actual mirror. We want to fix our hair and touch up our makeup, because we want to look presentable to people. We would be even bigger fools to allow a day to pass without looking into the mirror of God's Word so He could show us the things in our lives that need some attention. Make your time with God a priority and enjoy the peace of sweet fellowship everyday!

Lesson 2

Prepared Feet

Jesus answered, "If anyone loves Me, he will keep My word. My Father will love him, and We will come to him and make Our home with him. John 14:23

Yesterday we learned that we experience peace with God after we receive the forgiveness of our sins. This gospel, the good news of forgiveness, has put us in a position that allows us to enjoy fellowship and communion with the Father. It is in our time of fellowship and communion with God that He directs our steps. If we allow sin to build up in our lives, it interferes with our fellowship with the Father, and we won't be able to hear God's leading in our lives. We need to ask God daily to cleanse our sins, so we are ready to hear His voice.

The verse we are studying this week is Ephesians 6:15, "and with your feet fitted with the readiness that comes from the gospel of peace." Because we have received God's peace, our feet have been "fitted with readiness." The Greek dictionary explains that this word *fitted* means to have something bound to your feet, like putting shoes on.[1] The word *readiness* in the Greek means to be prepared.[2] In a more modern sentence we might say, "We have our shoes on and are ready to go."

I remember as a child running barefoot all day and not minding it. However, I recently attempted to walk barefoot down my driveway, and I hopped, hobbled and yelled "OW!" all the way. My bare feet were not prepared to handle the rough edged rocks. The trip to and from the mailbox took a lot longer and it was much less enjoyable than usual because I hadn't properly dressed. Had I worn my shoes, I could have walked briskly down to the mailbox, paying no attention to the sharp edged rocks. Being prepared for a situation makes all the difference in the results.

Our life is a spiritual journey, and each day we choose if we are going to follow God by completing the works that He has prepared for us to do or if we are going to be led astray to follow the world, the flesh, and the devil. In Ephesians, chapter 6 we are given the instructions we need to experience a victorious Christian life following God. Being properly dressed, with the spiritual armor God has provided will make all the difference in how many spiritual victories we experience in our lifetimes.

We were told to put on the belt of truth first because when we know the truth of God's Word

---

[1] Strong, James, *A Concise Dictionary of the Words in the Greek Testament* (Nashville, TN: Abingdon Press, 1890) #5265, page 74

[2] Ibid, #2091, page 33

Dressed for the Business at Hand

we can discern between the truth of God and the lies of the evil one. Secondly we are told to protect our hearts by putting the breastplate of righteousness on. This will keep our hearts solely devoted to the pursuit of God.

Now we are told that our feet are ready to go because we have received peace with God. We are ready to do everything God has planned for us to do!

Write out Ephesians 2:10. *For we are His workmanship, created in Christ Jesus for good works, which God prepared beforehand that we should walk in them*

God has specific marching orders for each of us. He has prepared tasks that only you can do. Let's look in scripture at some examples of marching orders that He has given to others.

Who was God giving marching orders to in Acts 8:26-40? *Philip*
What was he asked to do? *Speak w/ the eunuch*
What was the result of his obedience? *both Philip and the eunuch went down into the water and baptized the eunuch*

Who did Jesus speak to in Matthew 14: 28-33? *Peter*
What was he asked to do? *Come down out of the boat / walked on the water*
What was the result of his obedience? *he walked on the water*

Who received God's directions in Acts 9:1-15? ~~Saul~~ *Ananias*
What was he asked to do (vs. 15)? *Go to Saul in the street called Straight*
What was the result of his obedience? *Saul received his sight again and was filled w/ the H.S.*

Who is Jesus addressing in Matthew 9:9? *Matthew*
What was he asked to do? *Follow Me*
What was the result of his obedience? *He arose and followed Jesus*

To whom did Jesus give specific directions in Luke 5:1-11? *Simon*
What was he told to do? *Launch out into the deep and let down your nets*
Was he obedient? *Yes - He said "nevertheless at Your word I will let down the net for a catch"*
What was the result? *they caught a great number of fish and their net was breaking.*

I am enjoying this exercise so much! I could have you here for hours looking up different passages in Scripture. I hope you noticed that as each person received instruction from God, they obeyed, and as a result lives were changed for God's glory. Obedience to the leading of God in our lives always leads to changed lives! Sometimes it's other people's lives; sometimes it's our own lives.

Let's look up one last passage. In Matthew 28:16-20, whom is Jesus talking to? *the 11 desciples*
What were they told to do? *Go, make desciples of all the nations, baptizing them in the name of the Father and of the Son and of the Holy Spirit*

Were they obedient? _Yes_

What is the result of their obedience? _they baptized all the nations in the name of the Father, Son and H.S._

Oh Lord, we are thankful that your disciples obeyed You and taught Your truth to (all) nations! Because of their obedience, our lives have been changed, and we are grateful. Now that our feet have been made ready to obey, help us hear your voice and give us courage to obey so other lives might be changed.

And whenever you turn to the right or to the left, your ears will hear this command behind you: "This is the way. Walk in it." Isaiah 30:21

Dress Check:

Have you heard any marching orders from God lately? Has He laid a burden on your heart about anything? _____
_____
_____
_____

If so, pick up your feet and move out; there are lives waiting to be changed.

If not, pray today and ask God if your feet need some cleansing. Spend some quiet time with Him in fellowship and ask Him to show you what He has for you to do

Your life or someone else's life awaits the change that your obedience will bring

Lesson 3

The Way of the Feet

I am the Way. . . . John 14:6

Have you ever been in someone's way? I have been and it wasn't always the most pleasant experience. I have also experienced people being in my way, and I can't say those occasions were always pleasant for people either. These trying situations are opportunities for us to practice patience.

What does it actually mean to be in someone's way? I guess it could be when the courses of two moving people intersect. If they are traveling in the same direction when their courses

Dressed for the Business at Hand

meet, it means that one person takes the lead and the other follows. The reason we have to exercise patience when people get in our way is because most of us have an inborn desire to be out front and not following anyone.

This happens to me when I drive a particularly curvy road where I live. I know the road fairly well, so I can anticipate the curves, and I drive a little faster than someone who doesn't know the way. When I come up behind someone moving slowly, I have this itch to get past them and I look for the first opportunity to pass.

However, I remember one night driving through a particularly blinding snowstorm, straining my eyes to see the road in front of me. This time when I sighted a vehicle ahead of me, I was excited because I knew that His taillights could give me guidance. This person was also in my way; we were on the same path, and yet I was glad he was in my way.

What made the difference that day? _____

In one situation, I could see where I was going, and in the other case, I was unsure of the way to take.

We make decisions everyday about how to react to people and things around us, decisions about jobs and mates, decisions about godly lifestyle choices or worldly living, etc. Sometimes the right decision to make or the right *way* to go is hard to know. This uncertainty should cause us to look for someone who can lead us in the way that we should take.

Read Proverbs 3:5-6. If we want God to be the one directing our paths what should we do? *Trust in the Lord w/all my heart and lean not on my own understanding. In all my ways acknowledge Him and He shall direct the path.*

In Psalm 119, we find many descriptions of the *way* that we should walk. Look up the following verses and identify what God has given us as our taillight to guide us.

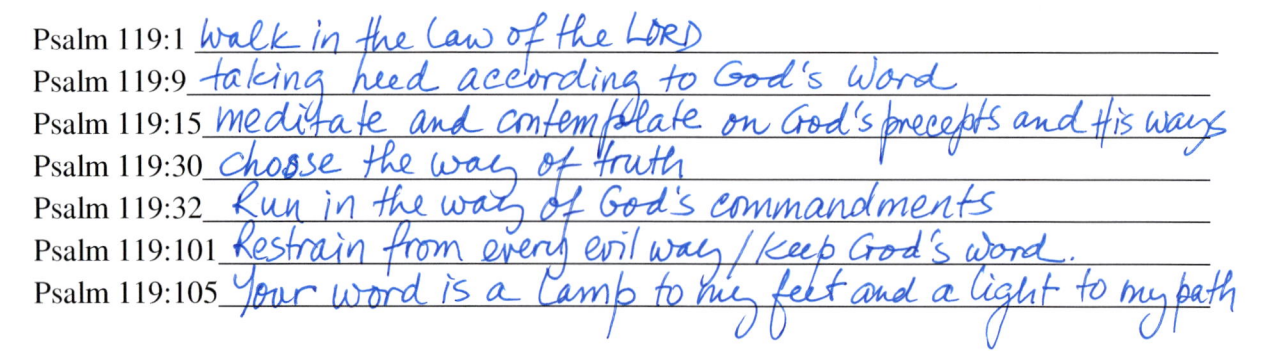

Psalm 119:1 *Walk in the law of the LORD*
Psalm 119:9 *taking heed according to God's Word*
Psalm 119:15 *meditate and contemplate on God's precepts and His ways*
Psalm 119:30 *choose the way of truth*
Psalm 119:32 *Run in the way of God's commandments*
Psalm 119:101 *Restrain from every evil way / keep God's word.*
Psalm 119:105 *Your word is a lamp to my feet and a light to my path*

If we want to be sure that our steps are guided by God, then we need God's Word, the Bible, directing our steps. The Word of God can always be trusted to lead us in the *way* of God.

The book of Proverbs is also filled with a lot of wisdom about the *way* that we take. Read

Proverbs, chapter 4 and write out the description of the path that wisdom will lead us on (vs. 11-12). _Our steps will not be hindered and when we run, we will not stumble_

Two paths are described in Proverbs 4:18-19. What is the difference between them? _The path of the just is like the shining sun that shines ever brighter unto the perfect day. The way of the wicked is like darkness. They do not know what makes them stumble._

I love that the path of the righteous is described first as a gleam of light that grows into the full light of day. I want to live my life so my footprints shine with the righteousness of God and if anyone chooses to follow my steps, they will be led straight to the presence of God.

In Proverbs 4:25-27, we are told that the focus of our eyes should be in what direction? _Straight ahead_ _Ponder the path of your feet (planned walk) (protected walk)_

According to Hebrews 12:1-3, we are to cast off any sin that is holding us back and fix our eyes on whom? _Looking unto Jesus, the author and finisher of our faith._

We will face obstacles along the way. Satan will attempt to divert and confuse us. The path may seem uncertain or blurred for a moment, but when we are unsure of where to go, we can open the holy Book and cast our eyes upon Jesus. When we seek the way that He took and we commit ourselves to following Him, we can be assured that He will lead us in the way we should go.

Take note of one last warning sign along the road. It's easier to follow when the way is rough and we are unsure of the way to take, but when the way gets smooth, we need to restrain the urge to pass the one safely leading us. If we pass Him and forge our way, we are in grave danger of getting lost along the way.

Write out Proverbs 14:12. _There is a way that seems right to a man, but its end is the way of death._

Let's avoid the path of destruction and instead follow the One who leads us to eternal life.

Since we live by the Spirit, we must also follow the Spirit. Galatians 5:25
If we live in the Spirit, let us also walk in the Spirit.
_N.K.J._

Dress Check:

Are you leaving a path with your footprints that would lead others to God? _____

_____

Are you following close enough to the One who is leading you so you won't lose your way?

_____

Lesson 4

Victorious Feet

I am able to do all things through Him who strengthens me. Philippians 4:13

"But I just can't!" Have you ever said that to God? Have you heard His leading in your life and argued about your ability to actually do what He has asked? I have done that many times. As God was drawing me to Himself, there was much cleansing to be done to be fit for His service. As He would bring specific sins to mind and tell me I needed to ask His forgiveness and forgiveness from the person I had wronged, I argued. I didn't think I could do the things He was wanted me to do. The first and the biggest argument lasted, to my shame, about three months. I had offered my mouth to God to be used in whatever way He desired and I wanted to honor Him in everything I said.

Before I was ready to tackle the jobs that God had planned for me, God reminded me that I had sinned against my best friend when I shared some confidences she had entrusted to me. This was sin, and God was asking me to apologize to my friend. When this conviction came to my heart, I wasn't sure if it came from God or if it was the devil reminding me of my failures. So I prayed for confirmation to know if this was from God.

After several months and many confirmations, I simply began to argue with God that what He was asking me to do was simply too hard. At that point in the argument, God showed me that I had crossed a line. No longer was I searching for His guidance, but now I had begun to rebel against His command. The Lord very clearly led me to Hebrews, chapter 12, and I knew that He was saying to me, "Jodie, if you choose to continue being disobedient to the directive I have given, I will have no choice but to discipline you." God's love for me would compel Him to chastise me, to bring me to a place of obedience. I cried out to the Lord saying, "I am willing." I chose to be obedient to Him and I made right the wrong that I had committed with my mouth.

My life has been changed by that one obedient act. God blessed me for obeying Him and has opened many doors of opportunity to use my mouth to bring honor to His name. I know those doors would have remained sealed shut had I not obeyed. I cringe to think of what would have been lost in my life had I refused to obey.

I began that argument with God with an unsure heart. I wasn't sure if it was actually God asking me to do that hard task. It was extremely difficult, and I wondered if I was misreading His direction in my life. Over the next few months, God reconfirmed in different ways that, yes, He was indeed asking me to be obedient by confessing my betrayal to my friend. When I finally couldn't dodge the fact that God was asking me to do something hard for His glory, I was held back by pride and unbelief. I doubted that God could or would enable me to accomplish what He was asking. My feet had become mired down in the sins of unbelief and pride, and until I cried for cleansing, I wasn't ready to move ahead for God.

Psalm 40:1-3 is a precious set of verses that illustrates this principle. In verse 1 we are told that we patiently wait for the Lord. What causes the Lord to turn toward us? *When we wait and cry to the Lord.*

It is this cry of helplessness that signals the Lord that we are ready to be obedient. I had wallowed in the sin of unbelief for so long that I was pitifully stuck in that mire and unable to get out in my strength. I had to cry to the Lord and say, "I am willing to do what you are asking me to do because I believe that you will enable me to do it."

Write out verse 2. *He also brought me out of a horrible pit. Out of the miry clay. He set my feet upon a rock and established my feet/steps.*

What a loving God we serve! When we cry to Him, He is faithful to deliver us from the sinful mess we have created. He picks us out of the mud, cleanses our feet, and sets us on solid ground.

Read verse 3 and summarize the results of feet that have been cleansed and set upon the rock. *He gives us joy in our heart — peo. will witness it*

Change occurs when we are obedient. **He put a new song in my mouth, a hymn of praise to our God** (my life will be changed). **Many will see and fear and put their trust in the Lord** (other lives will be changed also). That is victory to the glory of God.

If we are unwilling to obey Christ's leading because we are fearful, we may have believed whispered lies from the enemy. We need to tighten our belt of truth and expose the lies that are keeping us from trusting in the power of God to accomplish His works.

Write a summary statement of each verse as you read it.

I Thess. 5:24 *God's faithful and will do what he promised.*

It is interesting to me that in this verse we are the ones called, but He is the One who actually has the power to do it. If we could remember that Christ is the one who promises to do the work, we would cast aside any fear that keeps us from being obedient. He is all-sufficient for our needs.

Hebrews 13:5 *Be content w/ what you have. "I will never leave you nor forsake you".*

Whatever the task we have been asked to do, whatever the path we have been asked to walk; His presence will be with us all the time!

Dressed for the Business at Hand

Hebrews 10:23 _He is faithful to His promise_

If we are obedient to a promise from God's Word, we can trust that God will keep that promise. He cannot lie and He cannot change. His Word is always truth and He is always faithful.

What is the ultimate goal of our obedience? **Changed lives to the glory of God!**

Does this promise of victory mean that we will never experience difficulty? _____

What is the result of all God's work in our lives according to Romans 8:28? _All things work together for good to those who love God and are called according to His purpose._

God never promises that His ways will be easy with little or no affliction. Trials will come, but if we follow His leading, the result will always be victory, changed lives, to the glory of God. Romans 8:29 says that we will be conformed to the image of His Son. That is God's eternal purpose in our lives and that is good news!

Will He ever just give up on us and stop working in our lives? Phil. 1:6 _He will complete the work He has begun in us_

He promises that the good work He began will continue to be worked out until the day of its completion. We never have to fear that along the way God will lead us down some dark road and abandon us there. He will always be with us, working out His master plan for our lives.

There are also some wonderful promises in the Old Testament about the steps of the righteous man. As we look up a couple of them, celebrate with me that God guides each step we take along the path he has called us to walk. We can confidently follow Him.

Psalm 18:32-33 God—He clothes me with strength and makes my way perfect. ³³ He makes my feet like the feet of a deer and sets me securely on the heights

In uneven terrain He makes my step sure and He gives me the power I need to climb steep places I could not climb on my own. The view from those high places is breathtaking. He is a wonderful God!

Psalm 18:36 You _enlarge my path under me, so that my feet did not slip_ ~~widen a place beneath me for my steps, and my ankles do not give way.~~

This psalm is about God's help in fighting battles. He does not leave us to our own resources. When we follow Him into battle, He will make the way for us.

Psalm 37:23 A man's _step_ ~~steps~~ _ordered_ **are established by the LORD, and He takes** _delights_ ~~pleasure~~ **in his way.**

When we know God is leading us in a certain direction and we resist out of fear, we need to confess that fear to the Lord and accept His plan as perfect for our lives. We need to confess the source of our fear as believing the enemy's lie that God's plan is not the best. As we confess this sin of unbelief, our feet will be pulled from the miry clay and cleansed, and then our feet will be fitted with the readiness that comes from the gospel of peace.

There will be times in our lives when our way seems uncertain. We may be asked to walk in faith along an unknown path, yet as we walk in obedience, we can be sure of these two things:
- His presence will be with us always.
- Victory (changed lives) is His plan.

Accept the daily cleansing of God's Word. Lace up your shoes and listen for your marching orders. Victory lies just ahead!

For I know the plans I have for you" —this is the LORD's declaration—"plans for your welfare, not for disaster, to give you a future and a hope. Jeremiah 29:11

Dress Check:

Has fear or unbelief ever kept you from moving ahead on the path that God has asked you to walk? ✓ _____

Can you identify the lie that filled your heart with fear? _____

Did God have to chastise you to bring you to a place of obedience? _____

What was the result of your obedience? *Blessings, joy in my heart*

Lesson 5

The Most Glorious Feet

As I studied this piece of armor about our feet being made ready to be obedient, I could not help but notice the example of our Savior's obedient feet. His feet tread upon the soil of this Earth to personally deliver the righteousness of God. This gift of righteousness would only be available to us once the blood of the Deliverer was shed. Jesus came, obedient to the will of the Father, and he willingly laid down His life to deliver life to us (John 10-14-18). Write out

Dressed for the Business at Hand

John 17: 4. _I have glorified You on the earth. I have finished the work which You have given Me to do._

Jesus' obedience glorified God and it also triumphed in changing lives. In Luke, chapter three Jesus was tempted by the devil to step off God's appointed path and seek an easier, faster plan, but Jesus was not deceived by the lie because He knew the truth of God's Word.

Who was Jesus steadfastly committed to obeying (John 14:31)? _God the Father_

Whose will was Jesus yielded to in John 6:35-40? _Of Him who sent Me - the Father_

Jesus was unwavering in His walk. He had not come for His own purpose. He was not tempted to go His own way because He was dedicated to being obedient to the Father. The example of Jesus' steadfast feet on the path that He had been called to is something we should ask God to duplicate in our lives.

What was the Father's will in John 6:40? _Everyone who sees the Son (Jesus) and believes in Him may have everlasting life; and I will raise him up at the last day._

What did this mean that the will of God was for His Son? _Only through Jesus peo. will be saved._

In the Garden of Gethsemane we hear the difficulty in Jesus' voice as He accepts the hard task He had been given. Read Matthew 26:36-44 and record the answer that Jesus gave to God each time He prayed. _Not ~~my~~ as I will, but as You will. Your will be done._

He was willing to surrender His will to the will of the Father. His example is one we need to remember. When the day comes that God asks us to walk a difficult path, will we be willing to submit to God's will and walk it, or will we in disobedience look for an easier way, one that seems right to us?

Jesus never wavered from His path. He was obedient to walk every inch of the assigned path and by doing so He was victorious. His obedience has changed people's lives to the glory of God. I am so thankful that His obedience provided a way for the debt of **my** sin to be canceled.

Summarize Romans 5:19. _through Adam's sin we were made sinners so also by through Jesus' obedience we will be made righteous_

For the pure joy of adoring Jesus' feet, read Luke 7:36-50.

Who came into the Pharisee's house when she learned that Jesus was eating there (vs. 37)? _Mary - a woman in the city_

What did she do when she drew near Jesus (vs. 38, 44-46)? *She washed Jesus' feet w/ her tears, wiped them w/ her hair, kissed His feet and anointed His feet w/ fragrant oil.*

1. pharisee
2. the woman
What is the meaning of the parable that Jesus told Simon in verses 41-42? *The parable of two debtors. We are debtors in need of forgiveness.*

Simon, the Pharisee, had invited Jesus to his home to share a meal with him. His motives for inviting Jesus appear to have been underhanded, in that he had failed to honor Jesus with the customary water for cleansing his feet, and he also neglected the symbolic gesture of anointing his head with oil. Simon's inaction was a silent statement that he did not feel obligated to honor his guest.

We are told that a sinful woman came into the house that day because she heard that Jesus was there. When she looked at Jesus, <u>she recognized Him as the Messiah, and she also recognized her great need of Him. Her response was to lavish honor upon Him</u>. She approached the Lord with oil and began to be <u>overwhelmed with emotion</u>.

It is possible to think that she had carried the oil to anoint His head as the honored guest because Simon had failed to, or maybe she carried the oil to Jesus as a gift, the most costly thing she possessed. Either way, she stood behind Him weeping and eventually fell to her knees and began to wash Jesus' feet with her tears. After she wiped His feet dry with her hair, she kissed His feet and anointed them with oil.

She understood that Jesus had authority from God and she came to Him that day expressing her need to be cleansed.

What did Jesus tell those around him in verse 47? *Her sins which are many are forgiven for she loved much.*

<u>Those who have experienced a life full of sin's pain understand what it is like to live free from that sin.</u> Their hearts remember well the slimy pit of sin they were rescued from. <u>Those who have been forgiven much love much.</u>

Jesus spoke tenderly to this woman in verse 48 and said, "Your sins have been forgiven." In verse 50, He told her that her faith had saved her and that she should go in peace. He offered her forgiveness of sins and peace with God. That <u>peace is our most treasured possession</u>. It is this gift of peace from God that makes our feet ready to obey whatever God asks us to do.

Someday we will stand before the Lord and in His presence we will be compelled to fall to our knees, and <u>our faces will be at His feet.</u> There is no doubt <u>our lips will offer Him unending praise and thanks for His willingness to do the Father's will</u>; however, one question remains— Will He be thanking you for your obedient feet?

His master said to him, "Well done, good and faithful slave [servant]! You were faithful over a few things; I will put you in charge of [make you ruler over] many things. Share your master's joy [stewart]!" Matthew 25:21

Enter into the joy of your Lord.

Dress Check:

The Savior modeled perfectly the response that should be upon each of our hearts when God calls us to do a work for Him—"Not my will, but Thine be done." Has this attitude been displayed in your heart recently? If not, pray and ask God, to help you be willing. God's greatest works are accomplished by men and women who obey Him.

Forgiven Feet are Obedient Feet

This week in our study we have discovered that, because we have experienced the forgiveness of our sins and have peace with God, our feet have been made ready to complete the works God has prepared for us to do. We learned that the word *readiness* means prepared and we know that our feet have been prepared for some specific tasks or assignments from the Lord.

As we spend time each day in God's word, He reveals any sins that we need to confess, keeping us in stand-by mode, always ready to hear God's voice leading us. Feet that have been forgiven are obedient feet. I thought of the Apostle Paul as a biblical example of this truth.

Saul, as he was known before he was saved, was a man of great religious knowledge. He had been trained at the best synagogues and he was a zealous follower of everything he had been taught (Acts 22:2-3; 23:6). But having knowledge of God and being busy for Him does not necessarily mean that we are doing the right thing, because Saul was persecuting followers of Jesus!

Saul traveled from city to city tracking down followers of Jesus (Acts 26:9-11). It was during one of these trips that Saul had his first encounter with Jesus (Acts 9:1-19). Saul was blinded by a bright light and the voice of Jesus asking him why he was persecuting Him. In that encounter, Saul recognized the truth that Jesus was the promised Messiah. For three days, Saul did not eat or drink until Ananias came and laid hands on him and prayed for him. Saul's sight was restored, and beginning with Acts 9:21, we see Saul's sold-out life to serving Jesus.

Paul's heart was now set on things above, and his feet were ready to obey God's voice. The rest of the book of Acts contains the detailed accounts of the missionary journeys that Paul took. His heart was tuned to the voice of God and he was willing to go wherever God led him. It was not an easy life; in II Corinthians 11:23-28, we learn that Paul was beaten, flogged, stoned, and shipwrecked three times. He was constantly on the run and suffered many days without food or shelter. But even with all that suffering, Paul continued to follow God and obeyed Him.

Paul had been forgiven much and he had a grateful heart toward God. He knew that he had been saved from an eternity in hell, suffering for his sins, and this newfound peace he had with God motivated him to trust God and obey Him.

Another person that I thought of in Scripture who demonstrates a willing, obedient spirit is Philip. We are first introduced to Philip in Acts 6:5. He was chosen to help serve with the disciples because so many people were being saved that the twelve disciples were not able to keep up with meeting the physical needs of the people as well as preaching the Gospel. Philip, Stephen, and five other men were chosen to co-labor with the disciples. Stephen was the first martyr, being stoned to death. Philip's ministry is described for us in Acts 8:4-40.

Dressed for the Business at Hand

We learn that Philip had a wonderful, powerful ministry in the city of Samaria. He cast out demons and made the lame to walk. He proclaimed Jesus Christ, and the people of the town began to pay close attention to what he said. Many came to understand their need to trust Jesus as their Savior. A well-known sorcerer in the town came to know Jesus and he followed Philip everywhere. People were being saved, God was at work, and everything seemed to be going very well for Philip. Then one day an angel of the Lord appeared to Philip and instructed him to leave that vibrant, exciting ministry and travel out of the city to a desert road.

There is no indication that Philip hesitated over this new instruction; the verses indicate that he started out. He heard and he obeyed. I am so humbled by this man and his trust in God to lead him even when the way that God was leading didn't make much sense. I know myself and I know that when I sense that God is asking me to do something that doesn't make sense, I start to question God. I seem to obey better when I understand the reason why. But this is not what God desires from us. He desires that we trust Him and are willing to obey because of who He is and what He has done for us. We shouldn't have to know the why before we are willing to obey.

Philip left a vibrant, successful ministry to walk alone on a desert road. He didn't know where God wanted Him to go or what God wanted him to do but he was willing to go wherever God led him. As Philip walked along that lonely road in the desert, he met an important official who worked for Candace, the queen of the Ethiopians. This man had been seeking God; he had traveled to Jerusalem to worship God and, at that moment, was reading what the Prophet Isaiah had written about God. The Spirit of the Lord spoke to Philip and told him to go near to the chariot and stay with it. Once Philip got close enough to the chariot, he could hear the man reading the Scriptures and Philip called up to him, "Do you understand what you are reading?" The man answered back, "How can I understand, unless someone explains it to me?" He then invited Philip to come and sit with him so Philip could explain the passage in Isaiah that was describing Jesus Christ.

Philip's obedience afforded God the opportunity to reach a man of influence in the country of Ethiopia. The good news of Jesus Christ was rapidly spreading in the known world, and Philip was willing to leave a large and successful ministry to travel a lonely road for one man. Tradition teaches that one man returned to his country and introduced many others to Jesus. Philip could have responded to God's direction to go to the desert road with questions and a sense that this new assignment was a setback, but if he had, he would have been terribly wrong. God's plans are always so much larger and grander than we can understand.

After Philip's divine appointment with the Ethiopian man, God miraculously transported Philip to another city, and he continued to share the good news of the gospel.

This lesson is especially personal to me because I remember very clearly a time in my life when I was very involved in women's ministry at my church and I was teaching a large Sunday School class of ladies. I felt like I was on top of the world, doing the work that God had called me to do. Early one summer, I felt a little derailed when our 7th grade son asked if I would homeschool him the following fall. He was struggling with some peer pressure at school, and my husband and I decided that homeschooling for a year would be a good way to strengthen his faith. With the decision to homeschool came the agonizing realization that I couldn't continue with my busy schedule and pay due diligence to my new assignment. I reluctantly resigned from my teaching responsibilities but I was grieving in my heart that I had to walk away from something that I loved. I grieved in my heart until I heard the story of Philip being taught at our vacation Bible school that summer. I understood that God was asking me to leave my ministry for another ministry—one young man. What an awesome privilege to be asked to walk a desert road for the opportunity to minister to your own son. I quit grieving and began to embrace my new calling.

In the end, I homeschooled all three of my children that year, and in my estimation, it was an awful year. I was expecting them to appreciate my sacrifice in giving up all my activities to homeschool them and I expected they would love having me for a teacher. It was torture for them and for me. However, I don't consider that year a mistake or a misunderstanding of God's direction; I had just misunderstood the assignment. I thought this new ministry was about changing my kids; God was at work, changing **me**. He used that year to redirect my energies and my attention onto my primary assignment, raising three children to grow up loving Him.

I was busy doing good things, teaching others about Jesus; but by pouring myself and my energies into teaching women, I was neglecting my primary students, my kids. In embracing my ministry to women like I had, I was jumping ahead of my time table. That wasn't the page I was on, yet. I was still on the "raising godly children" page, and God used that year of my walking the desert road to show me that my greatest and most important ministry was within the walls of my home!

Thankfully, I didn't sense God's leading to homeschool the kids another year, but I did recognize clearly that God's calling on my life was to stay involved in their lives, getting to know their friends and volunteering at school and participating in all their activities so that I could be a strong influence in my children's lives. It is a profound and deep joy to watch them mature and serve God and follow Him. I am terrified to think of the consequences that might have occurred if I had been unwilling to obey God and walk the desert road He led me to. I didn't understand it at the time. I had small eyes with a limited perspective but I could trust that He could see where He was leading me and it was a good path.

This is one of my favorite lessons to teach to women because if I was teaching it now, I would interject a dozen more stories about times that God has spoken to my heart, burdened my spirit with something that He wanted me to do, and my responses to those directions. Sometimes he has pricked my heart to speak truthfully when a lie would be so much easier, or to return something that I had borrowed years before, or to speak to someone in particular about Jesus. I love telling these stories because sometimes we might think that God never speaks to us. Yet, as women listen to these stories, they laugh and they realize that God is still in the business of directing our steps; we just need to be tuned in to His voice.

These instances that I talk about are just small, everyday occurrences in which God prompts my heart to obedience. If I ignore His voice and His leading in common everyday opportunities to honor Him and represent Him well, do you think He is going to present greater opportunities for me to represent Him? Actually Francis Schaffer once said, "There are no big places or small places of service, there are only faithful people and unfaithful people." We will either be a people who hear God's voice leading us and obey it, or we will hear it and ignore it.

Dressed for the Business at Hand

Paul and Philip's feet were fitted and ready to go. Are mine? Are yours? When we sense God leading in our lives, will we yield to His wisdom and His ways or will we choose the way that seems right to us?

Not much of a choice is it? If we have known the forgiveness of our sins and we have experienced peace with God, our feet will be compelled to follow God.

Feet that have been plucked out of that deadly mire of sin and set on dry ground are willing to walk wherever the Lord leads them because they are thankful to be free (Psalm 40:2).

*If you have children you may wish to read the lesson on the feet fitted with readiness in *The Armored Baton* (page 153).

Week 4

The Shield of Faith

Day 1: The Shield Revealed

Day 2: Surround Sound Shield

Day 3: Without Faith

Day 4: The Seed of Faith

Day 5: Until He is All That I See

Dressed for the Business at Hand

Lesson 1

The Shield Revealed

For You, LORD, bless the righteous one; You surround him with favor like a shield. Psalm 5:12

In our study of God's Word these past three weeks, we have discovered the necessity of walking with the belt of truth buckled around us, girding our minds and allowing us to gather our thoughts and measure them against the truth of God's Word. The belt protects our minds from the deception of the enemy, it allows us to discern between truth and lies, and allows us to know with confidence we are following the one true way.

We have also examined the importance of having our breastplate of righteousness firmly in place, covering our hearts. With the righteousness of God protecting our hearts, we are not tempted to doubt God's provision for our lives; we are free to set our hearts on things above and experience the true satisfaction that only Jesus can give us.

Last week, we discovered that when we receive forgiveness of sins, our feet are plucked out of the miry clay and placed upon a solid rock. This gives us the freedom to walk forward in obedience to Jesus, completing the works He has called us to do. Obedience is an act of trust that declares we are trusting God's plans.

This week we will be studying the protection that God makes available to us along our journey.

We will be examining the extraordinary treasure of the shield of faith. We begin by focusing our attention on the shield. What is it and what does it do?

I looked at *shield* in the dictionary and noted that its basic meaning is to protect and that it can also be a piece of defensive armor. If a shield is used to defend a person, it means that as deadly or destructive objects are hurled at the person, the shield deflects the objects, protecting the one sheltered by the shield.

Let's take a few minutes to discover what God says about our need of a shield and the availability of one.

Who is our shield?
Who does the psalmist identify as our shield in Psalm 3:1-4? _the LORD_

Had you ever thought of God that way before? He is our protector.

The devil knows that God offers Himself to us as our shield and that we will be safe behind

Him. If we choose to walk behind this holy shield, the devil has no access to us! Doesn't that make you want to run behind the shield? Beat you there!

How is God described in Psalm 119:114? _my hiding place and my shield_
(refuge)

God will be our hiding place. We can run to Him when we face the enemy, and He will hide us and protect us, as a shield, from anything that would destroy us.

Read Psalm 144:2 and fill in the blanks. **He is my** _lovingkindness_ **and my** _fortress_, **my** _high tower_ **and my** _deliverer_. **He is my** _shield_, **and I take refuge in Him; He subdues my people under me.**

All those words describe the care that God offers to each of us. In an act of love for us, He will be our protector.

The protection of the shield is not a promise of a life without hardships, pain, or suffering. As we walk behind God, our shield, He sometimes leads us down difficult paths to teach us lessons in trust, obedience, His faithfulness, etc. Sometimes God allows us to experience pain or loss as He molds us into His image and strengthens our faith. However, we can be assured that the enemy cannot penetrate our shield, and if we choose to walk in the ways of God, His presence will surround our lives like a shield. It is this promise that allows us to have courage and hope in the midst of whatever hard times we face (Isaiah 43:2).

If we choose to step from behind our shield and leave the path that God is leading us on, we choose to walk exposed to the enemy (James 1:13-15). My desire is that each day we would choose to walk behind our shield so we never have to nurse injuries caused by Satan.

Whom does the shield protect?
God will be a shield to whom in Proverbs 30:5? _to those who trust Him_

This shield's protection is not offered as blanket coverage. This shield is available to anyone who wants God's protection and seeks refuge in God. He promises to be their shield.

This reminds me of the manna God provided for the Israelites in their wilderness travels. God's provision was there every morning, but He did not force them to collect the food. It was available to everyone, but as individuals, they had to make a choice each day to collect God's provisions. This conscious act reminded them daily that God was the blessed source of their provision.

God offers to protect us from the evil around us, and we must decide each day if we need His protection or if we are fine on our own. The obvious choice is that we need God as our shield and protector, but He will not force us to choose Him.

How does the shield protect?

In our strength we cannot protect ourselves from the enemy, but God never intended that we would face him alone.

In Psalm 28:7, the LORD is described as what? **My** _strength_ **and my** _shield_.

Knowing that the LORD God is between us and the enemy should give our trembling knees the strength to stand and follow God wherever He leads us.

Psalm 5:12 For You, LORD, bless the righteous one; You surround him with favor like a shield.

The Hebrew word used for *shield* in this verse means "a hook (pointed), also a large shield (as if guarded by prickliness)."[1] Another form of this Hebrew word means, "to be prickly, a thorn; hence a thorn hedge"[2]

Doesn't that bless your heart? Ladies, if we seek Him, He is waiting to offer us protection. He will surround us with Himself, and anything that comes against us will be pricked as if by a giant thorn hedge. We will be safely hidden inside. Seek His protection today. We are not safe a single minute if we choose to walk our own way, apart from God.

↳ *He hideth my soul in cleft of His love*

Dress Check:

Have you come face to face with the enemy lately? Have you wrestled with the decision to follow God or walk your own way? Did you ask God for guidance and protection at that time? If so, describe how He protected you? _____
_____

Have there been times in your life when, instead of choosing to follow God, you stepped out to make your own way and experienced suffering as a result? _____

Did you retreat to God, asking for His forgiveness and seeking the protection of the Shield?
_____

---

[1] Strong, James, *A Concise Dictionary of the Words in the Hebrew Bible* (Nashville, TN: Abingdon Press, 1890) #6793, page 100

[2] Ibid, #6791, page 100

Read Psalm 33:18-22. Write verses 20-22 as a prayer from your heart to your most glorious Shield. *My soul waits for you LORD. You are my help and my shield. My heart shall rejoice in You (alone) because I have trusted in Your holy Name. Let Your mercy be upon me just as I hope in You. Mercy = His unfailing love!*

Lesson 2

"Surround-Sound" Shield

The Angel of the LORD **encamps around those who fear Him, and rescues them. Psalm 34:7**

I am delighting in the knowledge that I have an awesome shield. God has offered to protect us with Himself. His power and protection are unmatched. This knowledge can't help but make you smile.

Read Psalm 115:1-11. *1-8 - Catholic Church.*

R.C. Church } Ladies, the world has nothing to smile about; their gods can do nothing for them. Oh, but our God, now that's a different story! He is enthroned in heaven as the God over all and He does what pleases Him. He has ears to hear us when we pray, He has eyes to see us in our need, He has a mouth to teach us, and He has hands and feet to help us in our distress. The fragrance of our sacrifice is a sweet aroma to Him. Our God is alive and powerful and He offers Himself to us as our shield and help. Oh ladies, we have **everything** to smile about! Are you smiling today? This lesson will make that smile get even bigger!

We delighted yesterday in our discovery that God offers to be our shield. The enemy cannot penetrate the shield of God. We can run and hide behind that shield. Today we are going to celebrate that God's shield includes much more than just frontal protection.

Read Psalm 139:1-6. Describe the Lord's awareness of what goes on in my life. *He knows everything abt. me and placed a hedge around me and laid His hand upon me.*

That is such a blessing to me. He is always aware. It is also convicting to me that He is so familiar with me that He knows the words I am going to say before I even say them. He is intimate with my soul. What other god is like our God (Deut. 4:7)?

What verb is used to describe God's presence in my life in verse 5? *enclosed*
A hand of blessing.

To be encircled by God. Think about this: completely surrounded, before me, and behind me. In the NIV, this verse is translated that God hems me in, before and behind. I love the verb *hem*. When I think of hemming something, I think of taking the raw edge of fabric and protecting it by folding it up under other fabric. God hems us in—He encircles me, **before** and

behind. In front of me and in back of me, I am protected.

An example of this hemming in Scripture is found in Exodus 14:19-20. Where had the pillar of cloud been positioned? *from the front* Where did it move to? *to behind them*.

He goes before us and He hems us in behind to protect us. Note that He also placed Himself **between** the enemy and His people. He is **before**, He is **behind**, and He is **between**.

Where does Joshua tell us that God is (Joshua 2:11)? *He is God in heaven, above and on earth beneath.*

Our shield is behind, before, between; He is God above and below. Is that smile growing yet?

Where is God positioned in relation to us, in Psalm 3:3? *all around me*

adverbs **Around, above, below, before, behind, between . . .**

Look at Psalm 125:2 and write down God's attendance in our lives. *He surrounds us forever.*

Indeed, he is **around, above, below, before, behind, between, and yes, He is surrounding me.** *circling.*

One of my favorite illustrations of this is found in II Kings 6:8-17. In this particular incident, the king of Aram was at war with Israel and he was angry that every attempt to ambush the armies of Israel had been thwarted by what seemed like an intelligence leak. The king summoned his officers and asked who was leaking the information to Israel. He was told that God's prophet, Elisha, was supplying Israel with the inside information. The king issued a decree to surround the tiny city of Dothan where Elisha was staying. The next morning when Elisha's servant woke and saw the city surrounded by the enemy, he was terrified and asked Elisha what to do. Elisha calmly assured the servant not to be afraid and then Elisha prayed and asked God to open the servant's eyes to the unseen spiritual world. The servant's eyes were opened and he could see the hills covered with angelic beings and chariots protecting them.

We cannot **see** our shield but we exercise faith like Elisha and know that God is indeed surrounding us and providing our spiritual protection.

The shield that God offers us is definitely a "surround-sound" shield. He is on all sides, in all ways. When we pick up our shield and walk surrounded by the presence of God, the enemy cannot harm us. His only hope is to convince us to walk without its protection. I am not listening to him are you? I am looking up to God, smiling at Him with watery eyes and thanking Him for being my shield.

Dress Check:
The presence of God in our lives is one of the most empowering truths we can understand. In Isaiah 43:1-3, we are told that God has <u>summoned us by name</u> and when we face situations that could overwhelm us; we are not to fear because God is with us.

Remembering His presence is all we need to calm our fears. Do you know the presence of God in your life today? Have you expressed gratitude to Him for choosing you as His own and for His attentive presence in your life? Take a few minutes and share with God, how thankful you are for His presence in your life._____

_____

_____

Lesson 3

Without Faith

Now without faith it is impossible to please God, for the one who draws near to Him must believe that He exists and rewards those who seek Him. Hebrews 11:6

[handwritten: he comes to God is that He is a rewarder of those who diligently seek Him.]

Each piece of armor that we have studied has encouraged me to walk boldly ahead for God, seeking Him and desiring to complete the works that He has planned for me to do. However, it is the shield of faith that has empowered me the most so far.

The realization that God offers Himself to me as my "surround-sound" shield is something that has transformed my mind. This newfound understanding makes me wonder why I have ever doubted God's leading in my life.

The reason you and I have both been guilty of doubting God's protection and His leading in the past is found as we examine the role of the shield a little closer. The word shield was defined as a broad piece of defensive armor but it also said this: "to cut off from observation; hide."

Each piece of armor that we have studied, so far, protected a specific part of the body. Can you guess what part of the body the shield is designed to protect? _the heart_

I have come to the conclusion that the shield is to protect our eyes.

If our minds are girded with truth, we are not vulnerable to the enemy's lies and won't be deceived into following him even if he's disguised as an angel of light. If our hearts are protected with the righteousness of God, the enemy will fail to tempt us into worshiping the things of this world. We will be satisfied with God. If our feet are cleansed daily, we will be on the move for God, completing the works that He has planned for us to do; we won't be a sitting-duck mired down in sin. If we choose to follow where God leads us with God as our shield, we have accepted His protection and we are out of the devil's reach. But instead of retreating, the devil attacks our one exposed body part—our eyes.

If we take our eyes off God, our shield, we might be tempted to look around us and complain about the difficulties we are experiencing. We might be tempted to believe that the path God has led us on hasn't been the safest one. We might begin to doubt God's love and His goodness. We might be tempted to walk away from our shield and try to walk our own way.

Have you ever looked at one of those 3-D pictures? At your first glance, and even at your first hard stare, you only see a hodge-podge of colors. Nothing makes sense, and the picture is certainly not one you would ever choose to hang on your wall. Yet if you can focus your eyes carefully into the center of the picture, the outside colors fade into the background and your eyes behold a beautiful picture that was hidden behind the chaos of the outside colors.

Life is a little like those pictures. Satan wants us to look only at the outside colors, the ones that don't make sense to our eyes. He wants to convince us that the picture he has for our lives is much prettier. God is saying, "You can trust me with your life. Look deep into my face and reflected in my eyes you will see the beautiful life I have planned for you." What you *see* in your life depends on what you are focusing on.

If Satan convinces us to shift our focus from God to the things that are seen with the natural eye, then we may begin to doubt that God's plan and His protection are the best. Our natural instinct when we focus on problems that seem large and overwhelming is to run. If we are hiding in God already, we just need to change our focus back to our shield and allow God to comfort and protect us. If we choose, instead, to run from God, we will have run from the very One who offers Himself to us as our shield. We will have exposed ourselves to the enemy's deadly aim. The enemy never hesitates to shoot someone in the back.

Write 2 Corinthians 5:7. *For we walk by faith, not by sight*

Do we choose to follow God only when we can see how things are going to work out? Do we obey only when we understand what God is doing? Do we walk with God as long as we can see where we are going? If we demand to understand before we agree to obey, we are walking by sight. Walking by sight is what the world does. They don't know any differently. We know a loving, merciful, holy God who leads us along the way. Do we trust Him enough to follow Him in faith?

What does Jesus tell Thomas in John 20:29? *Blessed are those who have not seen and yet have believed.*

It doesn't take faith to walk a path that we see in broad daylight. It doesn't take faith to follow a curve in the road if you can see where the curve leads. It doesn't take faith to believe in what is seen. It does, however, take faith to walk a path that is rough, dark, and unknown because Jesus asks us to follow Him.

Look at the following passages and write a brief summary of events in each situation. Ask yourself if the people had faith and if you see any evidence that people were willing to be obedient even when they did not understand God's plan? How did God respond to the people?

Exodus 16:1-11; Psalm 106:15 _they complained and He provided and gave them their request eve - he provided meat - morning - he provided bread._

Exodus 32:19-35 (note the "why" of their faithlessness in verse 23) _God respond by blotting them out of His written book_

Read Numbers 16. This is a little lengthy, but it is necessary in this study. These people were also faced with the choice to act on what they could see and understand or to follow God's plan which didn't make sense or seem fair to them. What was their choice, and how did God respond? _____

Deuteronomy 1:19-36. Summarize this account, taking note of both the faithless and the faithful people mentioned. How did God's actions differ toward them? _he faithless_

These have been examples of people who walked by sight. They had a human understanding in each situation and they chose to trust their understanding. They did not choose to follow God when things began to happen they did not understand. They couldn't comprehend that God's plan, as it was unfolding, made any sense so they began to question God's word. Their choice to abandon God to follow their own plans always ended with judgment. God was not pleased with their lack of faith.

Faith is choosing to believe God when faced with the unbelievable. It is when things don't make sense to us and we choose to follow God that we are displaying faith.

Hebrews 11:1 Now faith is the reality of what is hoped for, the proof of what is not seen.

Our hope is in the Lord, our shield.

Psalm 33:20 We wait for Yahweh; He is our help and shield.

Take your shield of faith and walk. Use it to shield your eyes from the enemy's attempts to cast doubts about God's protection. Keep your eyes focused on your powerful and trustworthy shield and you won't be tempted to drop the shield and run. God has great things planned for you just beyond what you can see. Walk on in faith.

Dress Check:

Have you discovered that as you have been following God your gaze has wandered over to the path of the enemy and that you have wondered if that *greener* path would be easier or better to travel on? Were you able to identify the enemy's scheme to place doubt in your mind, hoping to convince you to drop your shield and run? _____

Expose the lies with verses of truth. Write them on 3 x 5 cards and commit them to memory. Pick some favorite verses on faith and add them to your collection of verses also. Meditate on these when you sense the temptation from the enemy to gaze in his direction. They will help you to refocus onto your most amazing shield. You can trust Him with your life.

Write the references to the verses that you are claiming this week. _____
_____
_____

Lesson 4

The Seed of Faith

A man who endures trials is blessed, because when he passes the test he will receive the crown of life that God has promised to those who love Him. James 1:12

Faith pleases God. When we have faith and follow God wherever He leads us, it pleases Him. When we choose to follow Him in faith, it declares to Him and to the world around us that we *know* Him and that we *trust* Him.

God wants us to seek Him in order to know Him. He promises that if we seek Him, we will find Him.

Hebrews 11:6 Now without faith it is impossible to please God, for the one who draws near to Him must believe that He exists and rewards those who seek Him.

His desire is that we know Him.

God also desires that we trust Him. **Proverbs 3:5-6 Trust in the LORD with all your heart, and do not rely on your own understanding; ⁶ think about Him in all your ways, and He will guide you on the right paths.**

He is worthy of our trust. In all things, at all times, we can trust Him.

Our faith is an outward expression of an inward love. God's love toward me and His desire for me to grow in holiness will cause Him to allow trials to come into my life. Read James 1:2-4 and write down the benefits that God wants to develop in us during trials. _____
_____

Did you notice that God desires to strengthen our faith through trials? How will this strengthening occur? _____

Every day there is a spiritual battle for our minds and our hearts. Will we choose to dress ourselves in the protection that God has provided so we can walk in spiritual victory no matter the events the day may bring? Our armor includes a shield of faith to protect our eyes.

Will your eyes determine which path you walk today? Will you choose to follow God or choose the way that appears to be easiest? If we walk by sight, we may decide that God's way is hard and we might begin to lean upon our own understanding and leave God's way.

If we, instead, pick up our shield of faith, fixing our eyes steadfastly on God, we will choose to follow the ways of God, living obediently to the truths of God, following wherever He leads.

With our shields raised, we will soon discover that we can't see very far ahead, but a walk of faith wouldn't be a walk of faith if we could see where we were going.

What does Psalm 119:105 say will illuminate the way that we take? _____

God tenderly leads us along the way, step by step, precept by precept. We offer our love back to Him when we by faith take each step.

When we choose to follow God in the midst of a trial or temptation, our faith is tried or proven trustworthy. Each time our faith is proven trustworthy, our faith is strengthened. Trials strengthen our faith because they cause us to put this principle of faith walking into practice. Each time that God supplies the wisdom or strength to overcome the trial or temptation, I know Him better and trust Him more, thus increasing my faith.

Dressed for the Business at Hand

Are you a sight walker or faith walker? _____

What makes you think so? _____

Do you need to take a step of faith today? If so, tell God you are ready. _____
_____

Reach out and take His hand. He delights in helping us through every difficult step.

Write our Isaiah 41:13. *For I, the LORD your God will hold your right hand saying to you: "Fear not, I will help you"*

It is hard for us to fathom that we can consider trials to be welcomed events in our lives. The only way to accomplish this is to recognize the benefits that await us on the other side of the trials. James tells us that when trials come, our faith has the opportunity to be strengthened, and as our faith is strengthened, endurance is developed.

Endurance in the Greek means "cheerful, hopeful, endurance, waiting."[3] As we face each trial with faith, enduring the hardship, we allow the necessary passing of time for God to mature us. Maturity doesn't come overnight. A seed planted in the ground endures the blessing of rain and adversity of winds throughout a prescribed time in order for the plant to reach maturity. Endurance is that hopeful wait; it is the passing of time that is needed for the maturing of God's work.

Endurance is necessary for maturity. James 1:4 says, **But endurance must do its complete work, so that you may be mature and complete, lacking nothing.** We can welcome a trial with joy, not because it will be a pleasant experience, but because we know that we will be stronger and closer to maturity when it is over.

God doesn't expect us to figure out how to handle the trials when they come; instead, he offers us what in James 1:5? *wisdom*

God doesn't force His wisdom or His ways on us but He is available and promises to give us wisdom if we ask Him for it. God's only requirement is that we ask with believing hearts. If we are unsure whether or not God can or will give us wisdom, God's word says we are unstable. He says that we are like a wave of the sea being tossed up and down without any guidance. If we desire is to walk by faith, we need to lift our shield of **faith** not the shield of **I think so.**

---

[3] Strong, James, *A Concise Dictionary of the Words in the Greek Testament* (Nashville, TN Abingdon Press, 1890) #5281, page 74

If a person doesn't seek God's wisdom when they face a trial, what will be the result (James 1:10-11)? *patience — the crown of life*

They wither, and their blossom will fall off. As a plant matures, the blossom develops into the fruit of that plant. Inside each piece of fruit are the seeds to produce more plants! When a man ignores the wisdom of God, does he mature and bear fruit? _____

James 1:12 gives us the ultimate reason that we can face trials with joy. What will the reward be for persevering through trials? *the Crown of life which the Lord promised to those who loves Him.*

A crown of life! That even sounds beautiful. The reward that God promises to give those who persevere through trials is life.

When we ask God for wisdom to handle our trials, He helps us to endure the passing of time, and soon, immaturity is replaced by maturity. Then our lives begin to bear fruit, and that fruit contains seeds which God can use to multiply life many more times! That is something that can make us rejoice!

Trials will come; we know that. Are we prepared to lift our shield of faith and walk on? *Prov. 9:*

I can't help but think of Jesus and the crown of thorns placed upon His head. Yes, it was a victor's crown, a crown of life! From His obedience to follow God's way, no matter how difficult, we are the recipients of life.

Hebrews 12:2-3 Therefore, since we also have such a large cloud of witnesses surrounding us, let us lay aside every weight and the sin that so easily ensnares us. Let us run with endurance the race that lies before us, ² keeping our eyes on Jesus, the source and perfecter of our faith, who for the joy that lay before Him endured a cross and despised the shame and has sat down at the right hand of God's throne.

Dress Check:

Where are you in the maturing process? Can you accept the trials and the sunshine? Will you allow God the necessary passing of time to bring you to the place of bearing much fruit? Write a prayer to God, expressing your desire to bear fruit. Ask Him to help you walk by faith and not by sight as you endure the trials of life this week. _____

Lesson 5

Until He is all I See

The world was not worthy of them. Hebrews 11:38a

Faith is our gift of love back to the Father and it is a precious gift that pleases Him and brings Him joy. How do I know that? In Hebrews 11, God introduces us to some of His treasured followers. These people knew and trusted God and they loved Him enough to follow Him through valleys of suffering and death. By faith, they held their shield of faith in one hand, reached out for God's hand with the other, and followed close to Him.

Make yourself comfortable, open God's "brag book" in Hebrews 11, and let God tell you all about some of the most precious love gifts He has ever received.

Write the names of those God "brags" about in this chapter. _Abel, Enoch, Noah, Abraham and Sarah, Isaac, Jacob, Joseph, Moses' parents, Moses, Joshua and Rahab, and many others Gideon, Barak, Samson, Jephtah, David, Samuel_

I suspect that this is one list that God has continued to write. Can you think of names that God might have added more recently to His brag book? _____

I want to faithfully choose to follow God every day. It would be such an offense to God to have trusted Him to lead me this far and then, because of a hardship, begin to doubt His love and power, turn tail, and run. Oh Lord, I pray not!

The writer repeats a particular theme about faith in these verses: 1, 3, 7, and 8, 13, 26, 27. What is the golden thread that connects them all? _faith_

It doesn't take faith to walk where you can see. Faith is following God when the end is not in sight. <u>It is a confidence and hope in God</u> because we know Him and trust Him.

Pick one of the people mentioned in this passage and summarize their life and the path God called them to walk._____

The Shield of Faith | Week 4

Put yourself in their shoes for a minute and think of their emotions and the things that God asked them to give up for Him. Think of any opposition they might have received from family or friends. Do you think they experienced discouragement or bewilderment as they waited for God to show Himself strong on their behalf?

Do you understand now how great their gift of faith was to God? Can you see why God remembered their faith in this special chapter on faith? _____

Do you think if you faced the same set of circumstances that your faith would be strong enough? _____

Looking through this passage in Hebrews 11, I notice there is small group of people named in verses 32-35a. Not much of their story is told, but we learn they accomplished great works for God as they faithfully followed God. God replaced their weakness with His strength, and they witnessed the miracle of God's power against their enemies.

Another group of people mentioned in verses 35b-37 are not individually named. Did these men and women live to see the result of their faith? *they did not receive the promise.*

They had a sweet faith in God and were willing to follow Him. He looked at these dear sweet followers and asked them to trust Him in the ultimate sacrifice, their lives. They didn't know God's plans and they wouldn't live to *see* how God would use their gift of faith, but they believed and trusted their Creator God and were steadfast and devoted to Him even in death. Can you hear God's tender love for them in verse 38 when He says, "the world was not worthy of them"? I can only imagine the joyful welcome and embrace they received in heaven!

The men and women in this chapter faced the same evil and destructive enemy that we face and they remained true to their God. I am amazed. The enemy must have been relentless in trying to get them to doubt God. He must have tempted them to abandon God and choose an easier way of life. Satan must have used every form of deceit and trickery that he knew, yet they only had eyes for God. He was all they could see. They made the choice to find safety in their shield and they were willing to follow Him anywhere. Their beautiful devotion to God is the reason that God included a special page in His Word to rehearse their love story with us.

Ladies, my faith needs to be strengthened. I am ashamed of how many times I have abandoned my walk with God because I didn't understand why He wanted to walk that way or because I had focused on hardships and not on my shield. Walking in my own wisdom will always lead me away from God, and I will be an easy target for the enemy. If I walk away from the trials, I miss out on the maturing process that God is completing and I won't bear the fruit of life.

Dressed for the Business at Hand

Dress Check:
Does your heart sense this same desire? Will you write a short prayer to God expressing your desire for His wisdom when you face trials? _____

_____
_____
_____
_____
_____
_____
_____
_____
_____
_____

Ask God to remind you of this prayer the next time a *trial* rings your doorbell. Instead of running in fear, we can open the door with a welcome smile. We can joyfully expect that, by the time the trial leaves our doorstep, we will be a different person to the glory of God!

What a privilege to have Almighty God offering Himself to us, to surround us as a shield as we journey through life. We need to seek Him, and when we do, we will find His protection is all-sufficient. Walk confidently with God, **around, above, below, before, behind, between, and yes, surrounding you.** Complete the works that God has ordained for you to do. Who knows, He might add your name to His brag page this week!

"Come"

My shield of faith, it is the protection of God's presence in my life and my act of faith in following Him as He leads me. I don't follow because I see and understand; I follow because of who He is.

We have studied faith for a week and we will conclude with a lesson about it right now. But we will only be scratching the surface of what that will mean to your life because faith is an action verb that is lived out/acted out by each of us. I can explain what it feels like to run. I can explain how to do it, give you stories of people who have run, and even with all of that knowledge, until you actually run yourself, you won't have a complete understanding of the verb *run*. Faith is like that; we have to step out in faith and follow God to experience His faithfulness in our lives. His presence is real, and each time you experience a journey by faith, your understanding of God increases and your faith is strengthened.

My prayer is that as you have had a glimpse of what faith looks like as it is lived out in a life and that it will motivate you to press forward, seeking God and finding your shelter behind the shield of His presence, and that, in that secure place, you will choose to follow Him wherever He leads you, creating your own story and journey of faith. The awesome result is that then God can use your journey of faith to encourage someone else to trust Him and step out in faith. What an amazing thought!

Each time He leads us and we follow Him, He proves Himself faithful to us, and we see the power and the presence of God in our lives. Our faith is grown, and we agree with others in Scripture who have uttered the words, **Nothing is too difficult for the You** (Gen. 18:14; Jer. 32:17).

Steps of faith are steps taken without seeing the where or when or how, but trusting in the *who*.

Faith walking isn't for the faint-hearted; it is an exhilarating, adrenaline rushing kind of walk. Imagine that the impossible things are done because the presence of the Lord God Almighty empowers the weak to accomplish things they could never do without His help. That is some kind of walk!

Let's read about one of those amazing, unbelievable steps of faith taken by one of Jesus' disciples.

Read Matthew 14:22-33 and Mark 6:45-51. These are parallel accounts of the same event.

Even though the disciples walked with Jesus and witnessed His miracles, they hadn't grasped the full picture of who Jesus was. Their faith in Jesus was strong because He was with them. They didn't understand how Jesus performed miracles but they knew that, as long as He was present, He could accomplish amazing things.

Dressed for the Business at Hand

Jesus knew that in just a short time He would be physically leaving His disciples and He needed them to understand that His power and His presence were not limited by the physical dimension. He needed them to begin to understand what it meant to walk by faith and not by sight.

It is in this account that Jesus teaches His disciples a lesson in true faith. They would get a glimpse of God in Jesus and they would learn that, no matter how alone they felt or how dire the circumstances, Jesus was there and could help them.

Let's look at some of the details of this miracle.

The storm came

In Mark 6:45, we read that Jesus had told His disciples to get into the boat and to cross over the Sea of Galilee.

When difficulties come that almost overwhelm us, it is good to start by asking God to search our hearts and show us if the difficulty we are facing is His hand of discipline. If the Lord does not reveal any sin that we need to repent, then we need to trust that God has allowed the storm to come for the purpose of revealing Himself to us and growing our faith.

The storm that was about to overwhelm the disciples was not a result of sin; it was a storm that God would use to teach them a precious lesson about the presence and power of God in their lives.

Jesus was praying for them

In Mark's passage, we read that Jesus saw the disciples straining at the oars. The Bible also says that Jesus was praying while they were fighting the storm. He was keenly aware of their need and He was praying for them. His heart must have longed for them to call out to Him for help, demonstrating that they were walking by faith instead of sight. He wasn't physically present with the disciples, but He needed them to understand that His power was not limited just because they could not see Him.

> Will we look for him in the middle of the storm?

Romans 8:26-27 tells us that the Holy Spirit prays for us: **In the same way the Spirit also joins to help in our weakness, because we do not know what to pray for as we should, but the Spirit Himself intercedes for us with unspoken groanings. [27] And He who searches the hearts knows the Spirit's mind-set, because He intercedes for the saints according to the will of God.** Whatever path Jesus leads us on, we can claim as a promise from God that Jesus and the Holy Spirit are interceding on our behalf.

The disciples had obeyed God by getting into the boat and now they faced a storm which was keeping them from getting to the other shore. God wants us to look for Him in the middle of our difficulty. He wants us to ask for help and wisdom to endure the trial. He wants to reveal

The Shield of Faith

Himself! We can be comforted by the knowledge that Jesus was praying for them in the midst of their hardship. He does the same for us.

Jesus reveals Himself

In the middle of their distress, Jesus drew near to them.

Mark 6:48 He saw them being battered as they rowed, because the wind was against them. Around three in the morning He came toward them walking on the sea and wanted to pass by them.

At first glance this passage may be disturbing to us. Jesus wanted to pass by them? What does that mean? I am reminded of two other times in Scripture that these words are used describing God: I Kings 19:11 and Exodus 33:19-23. In I Kings, Elijah is running from Queen Jezebel; he has run for days. He is alone, hungry, tired, and afraid. God appears to him and says, **"Go out and stand on the mountain in the LORD's presence." At that moment, the LORD passed by.** The presence of God appeared not in a frightful wind storm, the earthquake, or fire, but rather in a still, small voice. God spoke to Elijah, comforted him, and strengthened him for the task that God had for him to do.

In the Exodus passage, the people of Israel had sinned by building a golden calf and worshipping it, and God had told Moses that His presence would no longer be with the Israelites. They could still go to the Promised Land, but the covering protection of God's presence in their lives would be gone. Moses begged God on behalf of the people to lead them. God relented and promised to go with the nation. At that point, Moses asked God to show him His glory. Moses wanted a glimpse of God! God told Moses, **Here is a place near Me. You are to stand on the rock, and when My glory passes by you, I will put you in the crevice of the rock and cover you with my hand until I have passed by (Exodus 33:21-22).**

Please do not miss the fact that God was present when He passed by. He had arrived to make Himself known to the people in need. His presence brought comfort, strength, and hope. I also can't help but picture that God told Moses that when His presence drew near, He would put Moses in a cleft of a rock and cover him there with His hand. I am thinking I might have been in a dark, hard place at times in my life and totally missed the comfort of God's presence and His hand covering me because I took my eyes off of my shield and looked instead onto the dark, hard rock around me.

When you are at your weakest point, keep your eyes open for God's covering hand; look for Him and rest in the comfort of His presence as He "passes by." He loves to turn our weakness into strength because at that moment He receives the greatest glory for the work that He accomplishes. If there is still a possibility that we can save ourselves, then the glory may mistakenly be attributed to us.

Paul said in **II Cor. 12:8-10 Concerning this, I pleaded with the Lord three times to take it away from me. ⁹ But He said to me, "My grace is sufficient for you, for power is perfected in weakness." Therefore, I will most gladly boast all the more about my weaknesses, so that Christ's power may reside in me. ¹⁰ So I take pleasure in weaknesses, insults, catastrophes, persecutions, and in pressures, because of Christ. For when I am weak, then I am strong.**

Dressed for the Business at Hand

His power is available in our weaknesses, and we have the promise of God that, when we draw near to Him, He will draw near to us (James 4: 8). He makes Himself to be found by those that seek Him (I Chr. 28:9; II Chr. 15:2; Pr. 8:17; Jer.29:13). Jesus longs to make Himself known to us in our difficulties in order that He might do the marvelous work of replacing our weakness with His strength. Don't miss Him when He comes.

He offered them comfort in the midst of the storm

As soon as the disciples saw Him coming to them on the water, they were frightened thinking that it was a ghost. They probably thought that with the wind and the waves fighting against them, things couldn't get worse, and now they thought they had seen a ghost! Jesus understood their fear and offered them comfort with these words: **"Have Courage! It is I. Don't be afraid."** When we think that we cannot possibly handle one more thing, Jesus offers us those comforting words: "Take courage, It is I!" He hears our cries and tells us to stop fighting, to stop worrying, and to stop being fearful because He is with us.

Jesus had come! He was with them and He told them not to be afraid. His words were like a calming balm to their hearts. Their hearts stopped pounding as hard, and hope replaced their hopelessness. Jesus hadn't calmed the storm yet because He still had another marvelous work to complete in their midst, but His presence in the midst of the storm brought peace and hope.

Peter saw God and walked by faith

Here comes the real adrenaline pumping part of the story. Peter heard Jesus speak, and right away Peter's fear of the boat sinking and dying disappeared. His fears vanished, and in their place, a bold new faith was born. Peter began to see with eyes of faith and he asked Jesus to enable him do something that was impossible, humanly speaking. He said, **"Lord if it's You, command me to come to You on the water."** Peter wanted God to accomplish a work in his life that only God could do. He wanted the glory of God to be seen in his life.

The storm was still raging all around. The wind and the waves were still crashing all around Peter, yet Peter looked with eyes of faith and begged Jesus to do a work in His life that defied all reason. He wanted to know the power of God in his own life.

I believe that the Lord was pleased with Peter's request based on **Hebrews 11:6 Now without faith it is impossible to please God, for the one who draws near to Him must believe that He exists and rewards those who seek Him.** One of His precious disciples was asking in faith for the power of God's presence to be displayed in his own life.

The Lord's response is simple. **Maybe** because His throat was choked with emotion and there were tears of joy streaming down His cheeks, "Come," was all He could get out. "Come," He said to Peter, just "Come."

Matthew 14:29 And climbing out of the boat, Peter started walking on the water and came toward Jesus. Christ's heart must have swelled with joy. Finally! One of His disciples had grasped an understanding of the power of God's presence in his life. Peter was walking by faith and not by sight.

As Peter walked on water, doing that which was physically impossible and strengthened by the power of the Lord, he began to look around. Oh, how we are just like Peter! The waves were breaking right around him, threatening to overwhelm him; the wind was pushing against him, threatening to blow him over; the eerie blackness of the water threatened to pull him under, and his eyes began to tell him that what he was doing was not possible and that he wasn't safe. Peter's heart filled with doubt and fear.

Haven't we all been there? As Peter's doubts began to grow, he began to sink into that inky black water and he cried out for the Lord's help. I believe that the Lord with His heart still filled with joy at Peter's eagerness to experience His power, reached His tender hand out toward Peter and laughed between tears saying, "You of little faith, why did you doubt?"

Christ's heart is filled with pleasure when we seek Him and choose to follow Him in faith. He delights to show Himself to us. In our weakness, His power is magnified. Don't allow the enemy to place doubt in your heart about where God is leading you. If he is successful in causing you to doubt, then he may be able to convince you to leave the shelter of the shield of faith.

Oh ladies, lift that shield high and let it extinguish those fiery darts that he is shooting your way. Keep your eyes on the One you are following and allow Him to empower you to endure things that seem impossible by human standards in order that you might glorify Him.

He calmed the storm

When Jesus stepped into the boat with them, His faith lesson was complete, and He calmed the winds and the waves with His words. All who saw Him worshipped Him.

Jesus had allowed a storm to come that had terrified and weakened them all. He then strengthened one man with a faith that allowed him to walk by faith instead of sight, and the entire company of people marveled and worshipped Him. That was His goal, to reveal Himself to them so that their own lives would be changed. Their faith was strengthened and they would be able to carry this message of who He was to others, causing others' lives to be changed too.

Jesus would be leaving His disciples in a short time; Calvary's shadow was beginning to appear. It was imperative, if the disciples were going to carry on the work of the Father, that they have a clear understanding of just who Jesus is. They would be asked to travel a difficult path and they would need to walk by faith.

The task for our generation is the same: complete the works that God has prepared for us to do. There may be hard paths to walk. Will we look for Him in the midst of our difficulty? Will we keep our eyes on our shield, the one we are following, and ask for strength and wisdom? Are we willing to walk by faith in order that the faith of others is strengthened? Will others be drawn to worship Him as we walk by faith?

Don't let the devil steal your faith. That's one of his goals, robbing you of your faith in our all-powerful God. Let's resist him and join the chorus of others in Scripture, **"Oh, Lord GOD! You Yourself made the heavens and earth by Your great power and with Your outstretched arm. Nothing is too difficult for You!" Jeremiah 32:17**

Dressed for the Business at Hand

But Jesus looked at them and said, "With men this is impossible, but with God all things are possible." Matthew 19:26

*If you have children you may wish to read the lesson on the shield of faith in *The Armored Baton* (page 157).

Week 5

The Helmet of Salvation

Day 1: The Deliverance of the Mind

Day 2: The Helmet Modeled

Day 3: The Obstacle of the Helmet

Day 4: The Principle of the Kernel

Day 5: Death Brings Life

Dressed for the Business at Hand

Lesson 1

The Deliverance of the Mind

. . . you are being renewed in the spirit of your minds. Ephesians 4:23

Have you ever stared at a 1000 piece puzzle before, wondering where to begin? During my study on the helmet of salvation, I've felt like each verse I've read has been another piece to a huge puzzle. I am now staring at all the verses and the truths that the Holy Spirit has taught me and am wondering how I begin to assemble this great puzzle so that you can see the glorious picture, the priceless helmet of salvation.

This first lesson is longer than usual, but it is the framework, or the border, of this puzzle. It is necessary to understand the principles of this lesson in order to fully understand the value of our helmet. So take extra time today; it will be worth it!

The protection that God offers with the helmet of salvation is so radical it will change your life. It has been revolutionary in my life. This piece of armor is critical for our success in completing the works that God has for us to do. If we have successfully placed all the other pieces on, and yet refuse to wear the helmet, we will not experience a victorious Christian life.

The penetrating verses I studied exposed the truth that I had not been wearing the helmet. I was still thinking like and being motivated in many ways by my old nature. I had not been willing to die to myself so Christ could live through me. I have begged God to allow me to understand this truth so that with great joy I could put my helmet on and do the work that God has called me to do.

Let's begin by looking at the name of this piece of armor: the helmet of salvation. When we put on a helmet, what are we hoping to protect? _Our head, our mind_

Certainly we hope to protect our heads from superficial injuries which cause immediate pain, but ultimately we are protecting our brains. We are protecting our minds, the part of the body that thinks and makes decisions for the rest of the body. We know that an injury to the brain can cause long-term damage, affecting our ability to process information. Even if the rest of our body is healthy, an impaired mind affects the quality of our lives. We wear helmets in battles, in sports etc. to protect our ability to think and process information.

Look in a dictionary and write the definition of salvation. _____

_____

The Helmet of Salvation | Week 5

In Strong's Greek dictionary, the word *salvation* is a noun that means defender.[1] It incorporates the idea of deliverance.

> ↳ saved from... rescue
> ↳ freedom from slavery to sin.

This last piece of defensive armor we have been given to walk victoriously for God is the deliverance of our minds, deliverance from the enemy within us—our sin nature. We were born with a sin nature and we were slaves to it. We thought and acted like our father, the devil. At the time of our salvation, God offered us freedom from the slavery of our sin nature. God adopted us into His holy family and has equipped us to live holy lives. Ephesians 5:1 tells us that we are to be imitators of God now. We have been changed and we are not to think and act like we did before we were saved.

Colossians 3:2 Set your minds on what is above, not on what is on the earth.

We were born with a sinful nature and have been a slave to it our whole lives. So how will we change the way we think now that we are saved?

Read Romans, chapter six.

We have been delivered from the power of sin and death in our lives

When we were baptized into Christ Jesus, we were baptized into what (vs.3)? _baptized into His death_

What has been crucified (vs. 6)? _the old man (nature)_

What is the result of the death of our old natures (vs. 7)? _freedom_

When we accepted God's gift of salvation, we were delivered from the power of sin. We are not enslaved to sinful desires that rage within us. The old sinful nature has been put to death, and a new life of righteousness has been placed within us. Because of this, we are not to offer any part of our bodies to be used for sinful purposes. We are to offer our bodies to God as instruments for Him to control in order to accomplish the works of righteousness that He has planned.

As we surrender ourselves to become the slaves of God, what benefit do we receive in verse 22? _the fruit of holiness and the end everlasting life_

When sin no longer has power over us, we are able to live holy lives.

The result of being set free from sin is what (vs. 22-23)? _eternal life through Jesus Christ our Lord_

---

[1] Strong, James, *A Concise Dictionary of the Words in the Greek Testament* (Nashville, TN Abingdon Press, 1890) #4992, page 70

Romans 6:9 tells us that death no longer had mastery over Christ. He had died once and could not experience death again.

Hebrews 2:14-15 speaks about Christ freeing us from the fear of what? _death_

We have been set free from the **power of sin** and we have been set free from the **power of death.** Before we were saved, physical death would mean eternal separation from God, and that was indeed something that was fearful! Because Christ accepted death's punishment for us, we no longer have to fear physical death. I think there is another principle of death being described in all of these passages, too. Our old nature was crucified with Christ on the cross. Its power has been broken in our lives, and we do not need to fear its death. We can let go of our sinful nature and its desires without fear.

A battle for control begins

This passage in Romans weighs heavy on my heart. If I have been set free from the power of sin and death in my life, why do I still make so many sinful decisions? Why am I still afraid to accept the death of my old nature? I want to be free from that old sinful man that still dwells within me, yet his death never seems to be permanent in my life. Just when I think I have accepted his crucifixion, I find myself in a hidden corner of my life kneeling over that sinful corpse, performing CPR on it.

Before we received the Spirit of God in our lives, we were slaves to the power of sin and it reigned supreme, unchallenged by our spiritually dead natures. We did not have the ability or the desire to fight against it. Sin's nature had absolute control. Now that we have received the Spirit of God, we have the ability and the desire to fight against that sinful nature. Now we have choices to make each day. Who will control my mind today, the Spirit of God or my sinful nature?

Romans 6:11-12 So, you too consider yourselves dead to sin but alive to God in Christ Jesus. [12] Therefore do not let sin reign in your mortal body, so that you obey its desires.

Romans 6:16-18 Don't you know that if you offer yourselves to someone as obedient slaves, you are slaves of that one you obey —either of sin leading to death or of obedience leading to righteousness? [17] But thank God that, although you used to be slaves of sin, you obeyed from the heart that pattern of teaching you were transferred to, [18] and having been liberated from sin, you became enslaved to righteousness.

In Romans 7:15-25, Paul shares a personal example of the struggle between his old sinful nature and the new righteous life he possessed. As you read Paul's struggle, do you relate to the war that raged within him? I did. What is the answer to the question he asks in verse 24 (vs. 25)? _Who will deliver me from this body of death? through Jesus Christ our Lord._

Romans 8:1 tells us that, if we are in Christ Jesus, we are not under condemnation. The Spirit of God has come to dwell within us and has broken the power of the law of sin and death in our lives. In my strength I won't be victorious over the sin nature. The power for this freedom and victory will come only through Jesus Christ as we allow our minds to be controlled by the Spirit of God.

A Spirit controlled life comes as a result of a Spirit controlled mind

Read verses 5-9 and identify the characteristics of the sinful mind and the spiritual mind.

Sinful Mind	Spiritual Mind
the fleshly things	the things of the Spirit
Carnal	life and peace
hostile towards God	

Did you notice that a Spirit controlled mind dwells on things that please the Spirit? It is also filled with peace and life, submitting to the will of the Father. It recognizes that God's wisdom far exceeds its own and is willing to live in accordance with God's plan. Tomorrow in our study we will see the characteristics of a spiritual mind demonstrated in Jesus' life.

Our position in Christ obligates us to choose to live with a Spirit controlled mind

Read Romans 8:12-18, and celebrate that not only has the Spirit of Life that dwells within us freed us from the power of sin and death in our lives, it has also ushered in with its presence the awesome responsibility and privilege to be called the sons of God.

Why are we obligated to live Spirit controlled lives (vs. 14)? _We are led by the Spirit and we are sons (children) of God._

What amazing title does the Spirit who dwells within us allow us to call Almighty God (vs. 15)? _Abba Father._

We have not been given a Spirit that enslaves us to fear; we have been given a relationship with God that allows us to call Him, "Daddy!" When we face the unknown, we don't have to run away fearful; instead, we approach our Dad and ask Him to help us through the situation.

Suffering will accompany a Spirit controlled Life because holiness is at odds with the world

As co-heirs of Christ, we will be asked to share His sufferings so we can also share in his what (vs17)? _in His glory._

Verse 18 says, **For I consider that the sufferings of this present time are not worth comparing with the glory that is going to be revealed to us.** Did you catch that? When we suffer, the glory of God

Dressed for the Business at Hand

is displayed to others. Paul said he considered the suffering he had been asked to endure as nothing, for the wonderful benefit of God's glory being displayed!

Suffering is a badge that identifies us with Christ

I Peter 4: 12-16 is a passage that reminds us again that when we endure times of trial and suffering, we are participating in the suffering that Christ was willing to endure for us.

Hebrews 12:2 tells us that Christ was able to endure the suffering of the cross because of the joy He knew would come. Was God's glory displayed to the world because of Christ's willingness to submit to the Father's will? *He endured the Cross for the joy that was set before Him.*

God promises to work all things for good

Knowing that we will face trials and sufferings, how does God's promise to work all things for good comfort you (Romans 8:28)? *Yes.*

Will these trials come without a purpose? *It comes w/ God's purpose*

Verses 31-32 tell us that God is **for** us. With God on our side, we are always on the winning team. Will God ever face a situation that is too big for Him? Is God ever going to abandon us? *No never*   *No never*

God promises that no matter the difficulty we face, we will never be separated from His love

Fill in these blanks from verse 35. **Who can separate us from the love of Christ? Can** *shall tribulation* or *distress* or *persecution* or *famine* or *nakedness* or *peril* or *sword*?

Write verse 37, because it is the answer to this question. *In all things we are more than conquerors through Him who loved us! overwhelming victory*

We are conquerors over *those* painful circumstances as well as all of these listed in verses 38-39: **For I am persuaded that not even death or life, angels or rulers, things present or things to come, hostile powers,[39] height or depth, or any other created thing will have the power to separate us from the love of God that is in Christ Jesus our Lord!** As a child of God, I am no longer under the slavery of sin. Christ's death on the cross has provided freedom from the power of sin and death in my life. As I accept in faith that my old nature has been crucified with Christ, I no longer have to think and to act like a slave to sin.

Freedom from sin's power means that I can choose the Spirit of God to control my life. The precious privilege of sonship has been given to me. Without fear I can face the suffering or persecution that comes my way, knowing that the glory of God is being displayed to all those watching me. I can know and trust that no matter what happens to me, I will never be separated from God's love. It was God's great love for me that purchased this costly helmet of salvation, so that I could be free from the power of sin and death.

Lesson 2

The Helmet Modeled

... My son, do not take the Lord's discipline lightly [*despise chastening*] or faint [*be discouraged*] when you are reproved by Him [*rebuked by Him*] ...
Hebrews 12:5

Yesterday's lesson assembled the border of our 1000 piece puzzle on the helmet of salvation. Christ's death on the cross broke the power of sin in our lives. That freedom from the power of sin and death in our lives allows us the ability to set our minds on heavenly things and think like Christ. Philippians 2: 5 (KJV) **Let this mind be in you which was also in Christ Jesus.**

In today's lesson we will focus our attention on the greatest example of one living free from the power of sin and death and setting His mind on heavenly things, Jesus Christ.

Read Philippians 2:5-11. What was Jesus willing to do so that God's glory could be revealed?
humbeling Himself and dying on the cross

Verse 7 speaks about Christ emptying Himself. This word *empty* means Christ emptied Himself of His rightful position and entered a world that would not give Him proper recognition. It's as if He stripped off His royal robe and draped on the cloak of humanity. It didn't change the essence of who He was; it just allowed the presence of Holy God to dwell among men. Yet earthly man failed to look beyond the cloak and see the Glory of God.

Which character trait would you attribute to someone willing to become a servant to others?
a. Proud **b. Humble**

In the Greek the word *humbled* has the idea of being made low or taking on a lower rank. A person who assumes a lower-ranked position becomes a servant to higher ranked people. The process of humiliation removes presumed prestige, honor, or power.

Christ, being part of the Godhead, could have rightfully claimed recognition, power, independence, prestige, etc., yet He emptied Himself and became man so God's Glory could be revealed to humanity. With the spirit of humility, He came to do the will of the Father.

Dressed for the Business at Hand

John 6:38 For I have come down from heaven, not to do _My own_ **will, but the will of** _Him who sent Me_.

John 14:31 ~~For the world must learn that I love the Father and that I do exactly as my Father commands. (NIV)~~ _But the world may know that I love the Father and as the Father gave Me commandment, so I do_

We are instructed to have the same mind as Christ, a humble mind. Philippians 2:3-4 says, **Do nothing out of rivalry or conceit, but in humility consider others as more important than yourselves. ⁴ Everyone should look out not only for his own interests, but also for the interests of others.**

In humility we lay aside our own needs or desires for the benefit of others. In humility we live out God's command to be a servant of others.

(margin note: Jesus / Others / you)

Colossians 3:12-14 instructs us to clothe ourselves with certain Christ-like characteristics. List the qualities that should cover us. _Tender mercies, kindness, humility, gentleness, bearing w/one another, forgiving. Above all put on love which is the bond of perfection._

Each of these characteristics is others-oriented. We are to live as Jesus lived, with interest of others in mind, not for serving ourselves.

John 13:34-35 is one of the first commands that Christ gave to His disciples in the upper room just before His betrayal: **"I give you a new command: Love one another. Just as I have loved you, you must also love one another. ³⁵ By this all people will know that you are My disciples, if you have love for one another."** The disciples of Jesus, the men who had lived and learned from Jesus and would carry Jesus' message to the known world, were commanded by Jesus to imitate Him by loving others. Love is not self-centered. Love is others-oriented.

With a humble heart, emptied of His own need of recognition, Christ demonstrated His great love toward us by saying to the Father, **not as I will, but as You will** (Matthew 26:39). He knelt before the Father, holding out His hands and empty of His own plans, and was willing to say, "Whatever You will." He was willing to do anything, go anywhere, and go anytime. He had come to Earth for the purpose of doing the will of the Father. He was able to surrender Himself because He knew the Father and He knew that He could trust that anything the Father asked Him to do, however easy or hard, would be for the purpose of glorifying God.

Did you know that Scripture records a prayer that Jesus prayed the night of His betrayal? He even prays for you (verse 20). Take a few minutes and read John, chapter 17. As you read through this prayer, pay special attention to the number of times that Jesus mentions God's glory.

He was willing to stretch out His empty hands and die on a cruel cross, bearing the sins of the world, so that everyone would have the opportunity to see God's Glory!

>Should we be asked to walk a road
>Much similar to His,
>Would we dare - hold back our hands
>Clenched in little fists,
>Refusing God to work His plans
>Afraid that it might hurt?
>Would we dare think
>We knew what's best
>And refuse the King of Kings?
>Open wide your hands to Him,
>Surrendering your all.
>His shining Glory bright will come
>And fill and light your life.

Christ lived a Spirit controlled life because He had a Spirit controlled mind. He was willing to lay aside His own needs and desires for the purpose of pleasing the Father. He had set His mind on things above and was not distracted from that mission when personal trials came.

He faced rejection from the very people He came to save. They argued with His teachings and called Him a liar. They mocked and ridiculed Him. They arrested, beat, spit upon, and stripped Him of His clothes. They believed His life to be of no worth and they crucified Him. Jesus was God in the flesh and He humbled Himself to endure the hardships, the humiliation, the rejection, and the pain from sinful men in order that YOU might see the Glory of God. Are you willing to be like-minded in order that sinful man might see God's Glory in YOU?

Anytime, Anywhere, Anything?

I Peter 4:1-2 Therefore, since Christ suffered in the flesh, equip yourselves also with the same resolve—because the one who suffered in the flesh has finished with sin— ² in order to live the remaining time in the flesh, no longer for human desires, but for God's will.

Dress Check

Spend some quiet time with the Lord, asking him to show you if anything is holding you back from a willingness to be like-minded with Jesus.

I Peter 5:6 Humble yourselves, therefore, under the mighty hand of God, so that He may exalt you at the proper time.

Dressed for the Business at Hand

Lesson 3

The Obstacle of the Helmet

But put on the Lord Jesus Christ, and make no plans [provisions for flesh] to satisfy the fleshly desires [fulfill its lusts]. Romans 13:14

Yesterday, we studied the mind of Christ. We learned that He was humble and willing to be obedient to the Father. He stood with empty hands in complete surrender to the Father's will. If we are to imitate that same attitude by putting on our helmet of salvation, we will need to adjust the size of our heads because the helmet of salvation is not one-size fits all.

The enemy's last great hope is that we will love ourselves too much to imitate the humility of Christ. Our old nature was crucified on the cross with Christ, and the power of sin has been broken in our lives. But the enemy's hope is that instead of celebrating the death of our old nature, we will fear dying to self and insist on carrying the corpse of our old nature with us, breathing life into it on occasion. He desperately hopes we won't notice the acrid scent of death in our hands.

Let's consider what a person would be like who has the opposite characteristics of humility. We get a pretty clear picture of this person by reversing the characteristics of yesterday's definition of humility. They would be a person who "who refuses to yield presumed rank, does not serve others, exercises personal power and expects honor." When you read that definition, what kind of person came to mind? _a proud, arrogant person_

A proud heart has no room for God. God wants us to love HIM with our whole heart, soul, mind and strength, not OURSELVES (Mark 12:30)!

The center of **pride** is *I*, and as long as *I* am the most important person in my thoughts, I will never experience a humble mind.

Proverbs 6:16-17 (KJV) These six things the LORD hates, yes, seven are an abomination to Him: A proud look . . .

Proverbs 16:18 Pride comes before destruction, and an arrogant [haughty] spirit before a fall.

Proverbs 29:23 A person's pride will humble him [bring him low], but a humble spirit will gain [retain] honor.

In its very nature ALL sin is prideful because it is the choice of me and my way over God and His way. Sin originated in the prideful spirit that Lucifer, the Morning Star, exhibited toward God. Read Isaiah 14:12-15. In this description of Satan's prideful heart, which two words are repeated in verses 13-14? _I will ascend, I will_

The Helmet of Salvation | Week 5

Did Satan   _✓_ proclaim these words from the top of his lungs?
    or
    _____ did he think them in his heart?

It's possible that not another celestial being knew that pride was growing in Lucifer's heart, but God did. This sin was an offense to the holy, majestic, and omniscient God who created all life with a breath. Imagine a created being thinking it had greater value that its creator. This pride-filled angel was cast out of heaven, forfeiting his close and peaceful relationship with God, and became a hateful enemy to God.

This fallen angel, the devil, will do everything he can to keep you from worshipping God with all of your heart. He has learned through the ages that if man loves himself, there is no room for whole-hearted devotion to God. He introduced sin to the Garden of Eden by convincing Eve that God's way wasn't the best way. He persuaded her to choose her own way, and the sin of self-love was grafted into the heart of mankind.

I had a conversation with a young lady who came out of a Satanic church, and she told me that people mistakenly believe that the Satanic bible encourages people to worship Satan. She said it actually encourages people to love themselves and to be unwilling to submit to any higher authority. I didn't know that, and I am not even sure it is true. But it wouldn't surprise me because if a person's heart is filled with self-love there won't be any room for loving God.

II Timothy 3:1-5 But know this: Difficult times will come in the last days. ² For people will be lovers of self, lovers of money, boastful, proud, blasphemers, disobedient to parents, ungrateful, unholy, ³ unloving, irreconcilable, slanderers, without self-control, brutal, without love for what is good, ⁴ traitors, reckless, conceited, lovers of pleasure rather than lovers of God, ⁵ holding to the form of godliness but denying its power. Avoid these people!

Underline each characteristic in that verse that results from self-love.

It's hard to imagine that list of sins being attached to anyone having even a **form** of godliness. Yet the reason they participate in these sins is because they have denied the power of God. What did the power of God accomplish for each one of us (Lesson #1 this week)?
love for another, honor, respect for another

It freed our lives from the power of sin and death. By faith we accept that Christ's death has forgiven our past sins and has assured us a place in Heaven with Him, but we often fail to accept by faith that God has also freed us from the power of sin today. The people described in these verses were denying the truth that God had delivered them from sin's power. They claimed to be God followers, but they were carrying around the corpse of their old natures and living according to its desires. They were living for the love of self.

Are you willing to say to the Lord with empty hands, "All that I am, all that I have, all that I will ever be, is yours?" Will you tell Him that He can do anything that He wants, anytime that He wants, and anywhere that He wants? Are you willing to celebrate your freedom from the power of sin and death or are you feeding the dying man in the corner because you are not certain that God is trustworthy?

As we follow the Lord daily, completely protected by the spiritual armor He has provided, the enemy's last hope is that you will fear dying to self. He hopes that if we are afraid to die to ourselves, that we will not let Jesus live through us and that we will insist on carrying around the corpse of our old nature, serving our own needs above the needs of others. If we are still holding the corpse of our old nature, then we won't have empty hands to offer to the Lord. We will be saying to the Lord, "I'm willing to do whatever you want me to do as long as he (our old nature) can come also." God's plans never include provisions for our old nature. The love of self and the pursuit of my "me" needs are never part of His plans.

The love of self causes us to change our focus from an almighty, loving, merciful God who is at work in our lives for eternal purposes to our own personal comfort and happiness. When this happens, we can be sure that our heads have ballooned with pride and that our helmets have fallen off. We will have filled our hands with our own stuff and we won't be able to pick up the sword of truth, accomplishing the works that God has planned for us to do.

And if the Spirit of Him who raised Jesus from the dead lives in you, then He who raised Christ from the dead will also bring your mortal bodies to life through His Spirit who lives in you. Romans 8:11

Dress Check:
Can you quiet your heart before the Lord and ask Him to show you if you are walking with your hands full of the self-love? Ask Him to show you the truth of His love and His utmost desire for your best in all things. Ask Him to awaken your senses to the vile smell that the sin of pride has to an holy God. Ask Him to fill your heart with peace as you peel your fingers back from that stinky corpse. _____
_____
_____
_____

II Cor. 5:15, 17 And He died for all so that those who live should no longer live for themselves, but for the One who died for them and was raised. [17] Therefore, if anyone is in Christ, he is a new creation; old things have passed away, and look, new things have come.

Lesson 4

The Principle of the Kernel

I have been crucified w/ Christ ... and I no longer live, but Christ lives in me. The life I now live in the ~~body~~ *flesh*, I live by faith in the Son of God, who loved me and gave Himself for me. **Galatians 2:20**

The Spirit of God has empowered us to be free from the power of sin and death. We are no longer slaves to our old sinful natures. We have the power to resist it. With the helmet of salvation firmly in place, we are yielded to our new nature, free to be imitators of God.

Jesus is our example of a life lived yielded to God. It is a life lived full of love, humbly serving others; it is empty of the pursuit of self. Having accepted the death of the old nature and its perpetual quest of self, we have clothed ourselves in Christ, and with the righteousness of God draped over us, we look at life not for "what can I do for me," but "how can I love **others** for the Glory of God?"

We are sure to experience many trials in which we feel like we have been unfairly treated or spoken unkindly about; in each of these situations, we will have to make a choice: will we hang on to the corpse of our old nature and insist on returning evil for evil or will we yield to the wisdom of God who loves us and let Him live through us, displaying His Glory?

Write Colossians 3:2. *Set your mind (heart) on things above, not on things on the earth.*

Verses 8-9 contain a list sins that will manifest themselves in your life if your mind is not set on things above. Write out the different sins mentioned in these verses. *anger, rage, malicious blasphemy, filthy language, lie*

When anger, bitterness, wrath, and rage display themselves in our lives, it's because we've believed the lie that the cost of dying to self is too high to pay. You can be sure that we are clutching the corpse and frantically performing CPR.

What does Jesus tell His disciples in John 12:23-26? *We have to die to self in order to produce fruit in our lives.*

For the Fruit
Dying to one's self, is an act of faith that will produce what in our lives (vs. 24)? *much fruit*

This is a paradox: How can dying produce life? We have to put faith walking into practice here. If we walk by sight, we will never be able to understand this principle and we will never know the fruit that comes from the death of self. Jesus uses the example of a grain of wheat in His illustration. Each seed must be planted deep into the darkness of the earth, and then, as a result

Dressed for the Business at Hand

of its death, life will spring forth. I cannot even think about this illustration without thinking of Jesus who was willing to die and was buried in the darkness of the tomb for three days, and from that tomb came forth life. Including yours!

For the Works
Jesus tells His disciples in verse 26, that if they are going to *serve* Him they will have to follow His example and die to self.

Ephesians 2:10 For __we__ are His creation (*masterpiece, workmanship*), created in Christ Jesus for __good works__, which God prepared __beforehand__ so that we should __walk in them__.

If we are going to accomplish the works God has prepared for us to do, we need to be willing to follow Jesus' example and die to self. People who love their lives and refuse to lay down their "me" needs will lose the privilege of knowing the life that God had planned to live through them. They are afraid to let go of the corpse and, therefore, cannot accomplish the works that God has planned for them to do.

For the Glory
Jesus is our wonderful example of living life free from the power of sin and death. Jesus was willing to lay down His life for others. What does John 12:23 say is about to be displayed in His life? __Glory__ Suffering occurs when we die to ourselves. Many times it is painful to re-nail our old nature to the cross. It will mean personal sacrifices, but when we suffer for the purpose of Jesus living through us, we can rest in the assurance that the Glory of God will be present.

Write Romans 8:17-18. __If children, then heirs, heirs of God and joined heirs w/Christ if we indeed we suffer w/Him, that we may also be glorified together. For if I consider that the sufferings of this present time are not worthy to be compared w/the glory which shall be revealed in us.__

What does Jesus ask the Father to do in John 12:28? __Father, glorify Your name.__

Did God do it (vs. 28)? __He has glorified it and will glorify it again.__

I Peter 4:13-14 are precious verses. What will be revealed to us when we endure suffering for Christ (vs. 13)? __When His glory is revealed, we may be glad w/exceeding joy.__

When we are insulted because of the name of Christ, what does verse 14 say rests upon us? __His glory__

The Spirit of Glory will rest upon us. Let's remember some occasions in the Bible when the Glory of God is revealed to mankind.

- God's Glory led the Israelites through the wilderness.
- His Glory filled both the tabernacle and the temple when they were dedicated to God.
- God's Glory passed by Moses on the mountain.
- His glory appeared to the shepherds to announce the birth of Jesus.

I know that there are many other occasions of God's Glory appearing, and each time that it appears, the presence of God Almighty is there in fullness. If we suffer for God, His glory will be present upon us, and others will see Him. Have you ever seen someone with the Spirit of Glory resting upon them? They radiate God, and the entire world sees it.

We have been given a costly gift, <u>the helmet of salvation, the deliverance of our minds</u>. Christ's death on the cross broke the power that sin had in our lives. Daily we must decide to recognize the death of our old nature, the part of us that demanded our own way. The power of God now acts on our behalf, enabling us to lay aside self-love and its desire that our "me" needs be met. We don't have to think as the world thinks anymore; we can accept with great joy the humility of emptying ourselves so that the Spirit of God can be seen in us as He works through us.

Dress Check:

Ask God to open your eyes to areas that you have not been willing to surrender to Him. Ask God to strengthen your faith so that you will be willing to trust Him in the principle of the kernel: from death, comes life._____

_____

_____

Lesson 5

Death Brings Life

"I assure you: Unless a grain of wheat falls to the ground and dies, it remains by itself. But if it dies, it produces a large crop." John 12:24

This week's lessons on the helmet of salvation have opened my eyes to the reason I have faced defeat so many times in my attempts to be victorious for God: I have had my hands full of my "me" needs and have not been able to handle the sword of truth effectively.

I know that it will only take you five days to complete these lessons on the helmet of salvation;

however, I have been studying, praying, and listening to the Lord teach me about His helmet for over a month. In God's infinite wisdom, He allowed a computer failure to force me to restudy and rewrite the lessons after I thought I had understood them and had completed writing about them. When my computer crashed, I cried. I had lost weeks' worth of study and writing. I felt defeated and just didn't understand how come God would have allowed that to happen. I have since learned he didn't *allow* that to happen; He *orchestrated* that to happen because I hadn't understood all the lessons He was teaching me yet. He knew that I needed to restudy and really get a grasp on all that this Helmet of Salvation would mean for us. Can I say that NOW I am so glad that was in His plans for me.

I am begging God to etch these truths about the helmet of salvation deeply into my heart. I want Christ to live through me; I want to lay down my old nature and walk in newness of life.

There is so much at stake; we cannot fail to learn this truth. Our culture vigorously promotes self and self-love. We desperately need the protection that the helmet of salvation provides.

Write Romans 12:1-2. _____
_____
_____
_____

We renew our minds when we spend time in God's Word. The Bible instructs us, and our minds begin to think differently. We take off the old nature and our old way of thinking and clothe ourselves in the truths of God's Word.

Jesus came so we could experience life apart from sin's control. His ways are at odds with our natural way of thinking. Jesus said that if we die to ourselves, then life will spring forth from death. He says that if we hold tightly to our lives, we will lose our lives.

Who set us free from the law of sin and death according to Romans 8:2? _____
_____

Through Jesus Christ, the Spirit of Life, we have been set free. Christ has come that we might have life!

Let's look back through the seven I AM titles that Christ identified Himself with in the Gospel of John. During our study on the breastplate of righteousness, we discovered that each of these titles revealed the sufficiency of Christ, and we learned that we could trust Him to satisfy our hearts' deepest needs.

I want to look at those titles again because I believe those titles also answer other questions we may have:

The Helmet of Salvation | Week 5

- Will He really **live** through me if I **die** to myself?
- Is there really **life** after the **death** of our old nature?
- Can we trust Him to give us life?

The first I AM title of Jesus is found in John 6:35. We learn that Jesus is our Bread. He will satisfy our souls, and we will never need to seek someone or something else to fill us. He will be all that we ever need. Write out the complete title that Jesus gave to Himself.
_____

He is the Bread that will satisfy us and He also gives us **life**!

The second I AM that we studied was "I am the Light of the world." This Light is the promise that when we follow Jesus, He will light our paths. He will give understanding and purpose to our lives. Fill in the blanks in this verse **John 8:12 Then Jesus spoke to them again: "I am the light of the world. Anyone who follows Me will never walk in the darkness but will have the light of _____."**

We will not live in darkness, searching for purpose or direction. The Bible says that before we knew Christ, **And you were dead in your trespasses and sins** (Ephesians 2:1) and we lived in the darkness of death, but with Christ's death we now know the Light of Life!

In John 10:9, we looked at the third title of Christ, "I am the Gate." This verse says that whoever enters through the Gate will be saved. (Saved - from the power of sin and death.) Verse 10b says this**, I have come so that they may have life and have it in abundance.** Not just life, but abundant life!

"I am the Good Shepherd" was the fourth I AM of Christ. We read this title in John 10:11. In this verse we find that the Good Shepherd lays down His life for His sheep. As I am reviewing with you these titles and seeing the promise of life in each one, it makes me want to cry. He promises to be all-sufficient to us and He promises us life. We can lay down our old natures and be confident that He will live through us. He has come in order that we might know life and know it to its fullest!

Jesus declares Himself to have power over death with his fifth I Am title, "I am the Resurrection and the Life." Lazarus had been dead for several days. His body would have already begun to decay, and Jesus showed His power over death by declaring His name to be, "The Resurrection and the Life" and by bringing to life a dead man. Christ specializes in replacing death with life. **II Cor. 5:17 Therefore, if anyone is in Christ, he is a new creation; old things have passed away, and look, new things have come.**

Write out the sixth I AM title found in John 14:6._____

There is no other way; He is the truth, and through Him we know life. **Psalm 16:11 You reveal**

the path of life to me; in Your presence is abundant joy. . . The longing in our hearts to know the presence of God has been met through Jesus Christ.

The seventh and final I AM is found in John 15:1, "I am the true Vine." Read John 15:1-17 and listen to Christ as He speaks to you. What does the Vine provide for the fruit that is attached to it?
_____

The sustenance needed for life. Life flows from the vine into the fruit. If we become unattached to the Vine, we lose the channel that life flows through. That doesn't mean we lose our salvation. If a watermelon is growing on a vine, and for some reason, it becomes unattached from the vine, it is still a watermelon. However, the nourishment needed to mature that watermelon is no longer available. It will not continue to grow and mature.

If a branch is not producing fruit, what will the gardener do in verse 2 to encourage the growth of much fruit? _____

I know that if God pruned my life, it would be painful and hard to endure. There would be death to certain parts of me that had kept me from producing fruit. But getting rid of the deadwood would allow fruit to abound. When we bear much fruit in our lives, who receives the glory (vs.8)? _____

What is demonstrated to those around us (vs. 8)? _____

Jesus tells us in verses 12-13, **This is My command: Love one another as I have loved you. **[13]** No one has greater love than this, that someone would lay down his life for his friends.**

Christ came to the Earth, laying down His life, that we might know the freedom from the power of sin and death in our lives. We have His example of humility to pattern our lives after. We must choose daily to recognize the death of our old natures and place the helmet of salvation on our heads so that we can walk in newness of life.

If we mourn the death of self, we stoop low, and the helmet falls off. Our thinking becomes like it was when we were slaves to sin. With the helmet of salvation upon our heads and our minds set on heavenly things, we will have the skill and the wisdom to use the sword of truth so that we fearlessly complete the works God has planned for us to do.

John 10:10 I have come so that they may have life and have it in abundance.

Dress Check:

Are you moving ahead today, protected by the helmet of salvation or are you still clutching to the corpse of your old man, afraid to lay it down?_____

It's not too late to offer empty hands to God and tell Him that you are willing, anytime, anywhere, to do anything. He has some marvelous works to complete through you, demonstrating His glory to the lives of those you touch.

Dressed for the Business at Hand

Anytime, Anywhere, Anything!

I'm Willing. Can He Come Also?

We have tightened our belt of truth. We know who we are following. We have covered our hearts with the breastplate of righteousness, finding our satisfaction in the only One who can meet our deepest needs. We have prepared feet, we are ready to obey, and we follow where He leads us, shielded by faith. And now, this week we have studied the helmet of salvation, our last piece of defensive armor. We discovered that Christ's death on the cross broke the power of sin and death and our old nature was crucified on the cross. We have been given a new nature, one that allows us to live in such a way that we can imitate God!

We have the Spirit of the living God within us, and this new nature thinks differently than the old sinful nature we were born with. With the Spirit of God within us, we set our minds on heavenly things. *heavenly minded to be earthly good*

We no longer worry about "me, mine and I" and we live in the humility of Christ-likeness. This is a life that is boldly empowered by the Spirit of God to do the great works that God has planned for us to do (Ephesians 2:10). This is a life that is lived victoriously, fully protected by the armor of God.

What happens that keeps us from living this new life in Christ? What is it that prevents us from knowing the victory God intends us to know? I think, a lot of people are afraid to wear the helmet of salvation. The helmet of salvation changes our thinking; it embraces the new life and willingly accepts the death of our old sinful nature. Many people are afraid to lay down their old, sinful, self-centered natures and pick up Christ's mantle of humility.

The helmet requires us to lay aside the familiar and embrace something new. For many of us, this is scary, so instead we just want to bring the old nature along with us. We want to wash him up and put new clothes on him. We hope that if we can change how he looks on the outside that others won't notice he's dead. We splash perfume on him in hopes that his decaying odor won't be sensed.

We might fool people, but God is never fooled. He sees the heart. And the heart of that old nature is desperately wicked and it's dead.

Until we come to the place where we hate the vile smell of its sin, we will continue to carry around our sinful, old natures. We are only ready to walk in the newness of a Spirit-led and Spirit-controlled life when our old nature has become intolerable to us.

One trap that we find ourselves in is that we can somehow overcome or tame the old nature within us. Sometimes we think
- If **I** just had more will power, **I** could resist the urge to sin.
- If **I** just knew more of the Bible **I** would be strong enough to obey Christ.
- Maybe if **I** attended more meetings . . .
- If **I** learned more verses
- 'if **I**'. . . 'if **I**'. . . 'if **I**'. . . do you hear the '**I**'?

Dressed for the Business at Hand

'I' doesn't want to die, it just wants a makeover.

Satan wants us to think that we can overcome our sin nature if we just try hard enough. He knows it will be a life-long pursuit. We may experience temporary periods of success, as we deny our flesh in an area, but on our own, we do not have the power to overcome its nature.

The only successful method of overcoming our sinful nature is God's way, and that is the cross. **Romans 6:5-14 (The Message), Could it be any clearer? Our old way of life was nailed to the Cross with Christ, a decisive end to that sin-miserable life–no longer at sin's every beck and call! What we believe is this: If we get included in Christ' sin-conquering death, we also get included in his life-saving resurrection. We know that when Jesus died, he took sin down with him, but alive he brings God down to us. From now on, think of it this way: Sin speaks a dead language that means nothing to you; God speaks your mother tongue, and you hang on every word. You are dead to sin and alive to God. That's what Jesus did. That means you must not give sin a vote in the way you conduct your lives. Don't give it the time of day. Don't even run little errands that are connected with that old way of life. Throw yourselves wholeheartedly and full-time–remember, you've been raised from the dead!–into God's way of doing things. Sin can't tell you how to live. After all, you're not living under that old tyranny any longer. You're living in the freedom of God.**

The old nature will not yield to **our** attempts to overcome it, because **Christ** has already overcome it at Calvary.

We need to accept by faith that Christ's death has overcome our sin nature

Galatians 2:20 and I no longer live, but Christ lives in me. Our union with Christ and his death on the cross is the protection that we need from our old nature.

Galatians 5:24 Now those who belong to Christ Jesus have crucified the flesh with its passions and desires.

Galatians 6:14 But as for me, I will never boast about anything except the cross of our Lord Jesus Christ. The world has been crucified to me through the cross, and I to the world.

We should be willing to wear the helmet of salvation daily, recognizing that our old nature has been stripped of power, leaving us to enjoy our new life with Christ living through us.

The work that God has planned for us to accomplish for Him does not include provisions for our old nature. As long as we insist on cleaning him up and bringing him along, we will not move forward with the power of God on our lives. God never empowers our old nature. Our old sinful nature is concerned with "me, my and mine;" God's plans require us to be concerned about Him and His ways.

Matthew 6:33 But seek first the kingdom of God and His righteousness, and all these things will be provided for you.

When we live in the newness of the life that Christ gives to us, we will seek the things of God first. Remember Christ's example, **John 6:38 For I have come down from heaven, not to do My will, but the will of Him who sent Me.** Christ could complete the work that God had ordained for Him to do because He did not seek to meet His own needs, rather He came seeking first God's kingdom. Following in Christ's example, we should be willing to obey God's leading and go anywhere, do anything, and serve anyone.

One time a few years ago, I received a rather abrupt call from someone from my church telling me that in lieu of an upcoming activity at our church and that I needed to immediately move the puppet stage and all the puppets out of the room they were in. I worked with the puppets at our church but I had never considered myself in-charge or responsible for the puppets. So, I was a little taken back by the immediacy and the urgency of the request. Okay, to completely honest, I was **a lot** taken back by the tone of the command. I put aside what I was doing and made the trip to the church and started moving the puppet stage and all of their accessories. My flesh was speaking rather loudly in my head and it was complaining about the unfairness of the request. I began to pray out loud "Lord, I want to have the mind of Christ and I want to be willing to serve anyone, serve anywhere, and do anything." I had to keep repeating this prayer out-loud to quiet the voice of my flesh. A few days later after the event at our church, I received an abrupt call from someone else who said they heard that I put the puppets in their classroom and that I needed to have it all moved out by evening because they needed to use the room. So, off I went to the church to move *my* puppet stage again. Guess what? I had to pray that same prayer again, out loud and repeated many times. It is hard to die to self, to take something that seems unfair or harsh and to react and respond with a servant's heart—the mind of Christ.

Let's look at a passage in Scripture that shows three people who wanted to serve God but came with their hands full because they insisted on giving priority to the corpse they were carrying.

Read Luke 9:57-62.

Whenever I had read these verses before, I thought that Jesus was being a little too hard on these men. What was so wrong with wanting a place to sleep at night, burying your father, or saying goodbye to your family? When I read these verses now, I see that each one of these men had a priority relationship with their old natures. They were interested in meeting their "me" needs first, before they were ready to follow Christ. In reality, each man was willing to follow Christ after they had first taken care of themselves.

These men were not rebelling against God. They were not saying to God, "There is no way I am following you in this manner." They were willing to be obedient, **after** their "me" needs were met. They had misplaced their priority. Do we do that sometimes?
- "Lord, I am willing to study my Bible today, but first I need to do these things."
- "Lord, I am willing to help on that committee, but I'm going to wait until someone asks me."
- "Lord, I am willing to go to the mission field after my children have grown up."
- "I will give that money you are burdening my heart to give, but let me save up a little more first."

One man in this story came seeking the Lord, declaring his willingness to follow. Jesus, knowing each of our hearts, told him that though the animals have a place to call home, the Son of man did not. Christ was telling him that there would be personal sacrifice involved in following Him. Laying aside "me" needs would be necessary if one planned on following Christ. Was it wrong to desire a place to lay his head at night? No, but it was wrong to use that as the measuring stick that determined whether or not he was willing to follow Christ. The

Dressed for the Business at Hand

desire of this man's heart to follow Christ was right, but his priority was satisfying the comfort of himself.

The next man Christ beckoned with the command "Follow me." This man was also willing to be obedient . . . in a little while...on his own time table. He needed to tend to some other business first. He had heard the distinct call of God in His life, and he said, "Let me take care of my "me" needs first. Then I will be back to follow you." His priority was himself.

The third man may have been a witness to the previous two conversations and he called out to Christ, "I will follow you, Lord." This man had come to the place in his heart in which he had addressed Jesus as "Lord." He was acknowledging the ownership that Christ had over His life, and yet he too said, "First let me go back and say good-bye to my family." The sin is not in what he desired to do; the sin was the priority placed upon what the man desired.

Each man, while holding tightly to his self-centered and self-motivated old nature, desired to follow Christ and to be used by Him, but we cannot serve Christ if we insist on bringing the corpse. We will never know victory.

There are two compelling reasons that we should be willing to lay aside our old natures and follow Christ. Because of who He is and because of what He has done for us.

Who is He?

Colossians 1:15-20 He is the image of the invisible God, the firstborn over all creation. [16] For everything was created by Him, in heaven and on earth, the visible and the invisible, whether thrones or dominions or rulers or authorities— all things have been created through Him and for Him. [17] He is before all things, and by Him all things hold together. [18] He is also the head of the body, the church; He is the beginning, the firstborn from the dead, so that He might come to have first place in everything. [19] For God was pleased to have all His fullness dwell in Him, [20] and through Him to reconcile everything to Himself by making peace through the blood of His cross — whether things on earth or things in heaven.

He is the creator of all things, the head of the body, the Church. The head's role in a body is to direct the functions of the members of its body. The member's role in the body is to heed the direction of the head. When the members of the body begin to say to the head, "I will do what you are asking me to do, in a few minutes, after I have finished what I want to do," the body is in trouble.

Each member's priority should be to the head. Our priority should be to our head, Jesus Christ. As individual members of the body of Christ, we do not have the right or the authority to become self-centered. When we do, we can be sure that we are holding on to the corpse of our self-centered, old nature.

Revelation 19:16 And He has a name written on His robe and on His thigh: KING OF KINGS AND LORD OF LORDS.

There is no one with more authority than Jesus Christ. He is the King over all kings and the Lord over all lords. A lord is someone who is master to, ruler over, or owner of something. As followers of Jesus Christ, we need to recognize Him as our Lord. As Lord, He has all authority over what is His.

Philippians 2:10 so that at the name of Jesus every knee will bow — of those who are in heaven and on earth and under the earth —

Who is He? Almighty and loving God, Creator of all things, the head of the body, the Lord of lords. We should be motivated and eager to accept the death of our old, sinful, self-centered natures because **JESUS** wants to live through us!

What has He done for us?

We should also be eager to lay aside our own self-centered agendas and follow Christ because of what He has done for us. **I Corinthians 6:19 Don't you know that your body is a sanctuary of the Holy Spirit who is in you, whom you have from God? You are not your own . . .**

He purchased us from the slave market of sin. He gave His life in order that we might have life, and His death broke the power that sin and death had over us. **John 10:10 A thief comes only to steal and to kill and to destroy. I have come so that they may have life and have it in abundance.** We can never overcome or clean up our self-centered sin nature. Its death came by the death of Jesus Christ. We need to accept by faith each day that our old nature has been crucified with Christ on the tree. We do not have to be slaves to sin anymore.

If we believe that dying to one's self is to be feared or grieved, then we have been deceived by the enemy of God. Sometimes we are afraid to accept its death and live in the newness of life, so in our pursuit of God, we drag along the corpse of our old nature. We come, like the three men in our scripture passage, with our priorities all mixed up. We want to follow Christ, but we want to take care of the corpse too. If when we come to Christ, our priority agenda is still all about "me, my, and I," then our hands will already be full and we will not be available to complete the works that He has prepared for us to do.

There is no record in Scripture that any of these men in Luke 9 chose the priority of Christ. Actually the next verse in Scripture says this: **After this, the Lord appointed 70 others, and He sent them ahead of Him in pairs to every town and place where He Himself was about to go.** The Lord picked 72 **other** people to work for Him. I see that these three men with willing hearts lost out on completing the works that God had planned for them to do because they were too afraid to wear the helmet of salvation. They were not willing to die to self in order to let Christ live through them.

We do not want to be like these men. If we are still clinging to our old natures (I, me, myself), we need to beg God to make that sin nature intolerable to us. We need to ask God to give us the courage we need to accept its daily crucifixion, and we need to ask the Spirit of God to live through us. Only then are we prepared to fully live as God desires us to!

*If you have children you may wish to read the lesson on the helmet of salvation in *The Armored Baton* (page 159).

Week 6

The Sword of the Spirit

Day 1: What Sword?

Day 2: The Power of the Sword

Day 3: The Purpose of the Sword

Day 4: Possessing the Sword

Day 5: Swordless

Lesson 1

What Sword?

They were astonished at His teaching because, unlike the scribes, He was teaching them as one having authority. Mark 1:22

This is a very exciting day for us in this study. God has provided everything we need to be protected from the enemy as we live completing the works that God has planned for us. We have studied the pieces, and we have fully dressed ourselves in our defensive armor. Make a habit of praying daily for the protection that each piece offers.

If you ever find yourself -
- Wandering without spiritual purpose, being tossed to and fro, feeling alone, avoiding God
- Pursuing the things of this world, trying to find satisfaction in created things
- Mired down in sin, unwilling to repent, refusing to obey
- Forging your own way apart from God, walking by sight
- Thinking like your old man, concerned with your "me" needs

- ask God to show you where your armor has been compromised and ask Him to give you the grace and the courage to pick it back up and redress yourself.

Once we are fully protected with our defensive armor, our hands are available to pick up the sword of the spirit. This sword is another of God's gifts to us; it is powerful and needs to be used with great care. This is the sword that we will use to defeat the enemy in our personal spiritual battles and as we try to rescue people from the bondage of sin and death. This is a celebration day because God's sword is always victorious!

So what is the sword?

I looked up the word *sword* in a dictionary and discovered that it is an offensive weapon with a long blade used in warfare for the purpose of cutting or thrusting. It also says that it is recognized as a symbol of honor and authority.

What does Ephesians 6:17 tell us the sword of the spirit is? _the Word of God_

God's Word was the essence of our first piece of armor, the belt of truth; here we see it again as the essence of our last piece of armor. We are hemmed in and protected by truth.

What does Jesus say has been given to Him in Matthew 28:18? _all authority_

Dressed for the Business at Hand

What three things does He command His disciples to do in verses 19-20?
Go, make disciples and baptize in the name of Father, Son & HS teach to observe all things that I have commanded

When the disciples obey this command of Christ's, whose authority do they operate under?
Jesus' authority

This is huge to me because I know that I have no authority against the enemy on my own. But having identified myself with Jesus' death on the cross and having received His forgiveness, I have been given His robe of righteousness. I am now clothed in the righteousness of Jesus Christ. When I am fighting spiritual battles, clothed in the armor of God, the enemy shouldn't see me, he should see the authority of Jesus, and that, my friends, will give him cause to flee.

Jesus stood firmly against the devil, exposing his lies and completing the works that God had given Him to do. Jesus defeated Satan on the cross. Sin's power in the lives of men has been broken and someday soon Jesus will return to this Earth as the King of Kings and Lord of Lords. Satan's time of being the prince of the power of the air is short because Christ's victory has already been won.

Acts 1:8 But you will receive *power* **when the Holy Spirit has come on you, and you will be My** *witness* **in Jerusalem, in all Judea and Samaria, and to the ends of the earth.**
to live holy lives

Our uniforms have been changed, we are in God's army now, and we are armed with His power and authority. Because of that, we are to live holy and righteous lives as we as tell others about Jesus.

According to John 14:26, what is one of the reasons that Jesus said that He would send the Comforter *Helper* to us? *to bring to rememberance of everything He has told us*

What title is given to the Holy Spirit of God in John 16:13? *the Spirit of truth*

With the Spirit of God dwelling in us, we are able to understand the Scriptures. His Spirit will teach us all things and He will guide us into all truth. We have been given the inspired Word of God to share with the world. We are to be living, speaking witnesses of what God's power has accomplished in our lives.

Read I Corinthians 2:6-16 and write out the privileges that are ours because the Holy Spirit dwells within us. *We understand God's deep secrets. We can compare spiritual things w/spiritual. We have the mind of Christ. We have spiritual discernment*

The wisdom of God dwells in us, giving us understanding to the deep things of God. Without God's Spirit enlightening and teaching us, God's Words would seem like foolishness.

In Mark 13:3-4, Peter, James, John and Andrew began to question Jesus about the end times. They wanted to know when to be ready for the hard time that Jesus had described would be coming. In the middle of Jesus' answer to them, He told them to expect persecution because of their testimony about Christ and He also told them that they would be arrested and handed over to speak before the governors and kings. Why did He tell them not to worry about what they would say (vs.11)? *He would put the words in our mouth.*

The Spirit of God dwells within us, instructing and guiding us in what to say.

Ladies, I do hope you have discovered today that having this sword of truth means that we can speak about the things of God because we speak by the authority of Jesus Christ. We are His flesh-and-blood witnesses, and He has given us power and authority to go to all nations teaching them God's Word and making them disciples. And the whole time we are doing this, we are completing the works that God has prepared for us to do

We need to believe God's Word. **Romans 8:37 No, in all these things we are more than victorious** *(Conquerors)* **through Him who loved us.**

We are fully protected in the armor of God, we have the authority of the sword in our hands, and we can march out with confidence to complete anything that God has prepared for us to do. I think I see a swagger in your step! March on, dear lady, God is with you.

Dress Check:
Were you a witness to anyone this week? _____

Do you have enough of God's Word in your heart that it comes out your mouth? _____
_____

Have you learned anything in this lesson that will make a difference in your walk this week?
_____
_____
_____
_____

God is light and there is no darkness, and Satan is darkness and there is no light. When you come face to face with the enemy and you are clothed in the brightness of the righteousness of God and you speak God's words using the sword of truth, Satan will flee into the shadows.

Dressed for the Business at Hand

Lesson 2

The Power of the Sword

Genesis 1:3a Then God said . . .

Dear ladies, I hope your spirit was filled with excitement yesterday as you began to imagine God's power working through your life as you accomplish the works that He has planned for you to do. We work under His authority and with His power. I hope that gives you courage to step out in faith and follow God wherever He leads you, using your sword to bring truth to those in need.

According to Hebrews 4:12, what power does that sword of truth have? *the discerner of the thoughts*

List the qualities attributed to the Word of God in Hebrews 4:12. *living and powerful, sharper than any two-edged sword, piercing to the division of soul and spirit, joint and marrow*

Let's look at each of these qualities.

1. **Living** → *it interacts*

   The Word of God is alive. When I looked up the word *live* in the dictionary, one definition that it gave was "not typeset yet." That created a word picture in my mind of a live-action play or interview; the words that the people would speak had not been typed out as a script. The idea of a live performance means that as interaction takes place between the parties, the outcome is determined by the words that are spoken.

   God's Word is like that. It is alive and as each person in each generation interacts with the words of God, the words speak to the needs of each individual heart. The Word of God is not a stale piece of copy that was typeset many years ago; God's words have life and they interact individually with each person.

2. **Active** (NIV) **Powerful** (KJV)

   You are going to love this word! The Greek word is *energes* and is defined as, "refers to energy, engaged in work, active, powerful." When this word is used in classical Greek writings, it is used almost exclusively as a medical term referring to medicinal treatment.[1]

---

[1] Zodhiates, Spiros, ed. *The Hebrew-Greek Key Word Study Bible* (Chattanooga, TN: AMG Publishers, 1996) #1756, page 1832

The Sword of the Spirit | Week 6

Don't you just love that! God has said that His Word is alive, interacting with each person who reads it, and now it is like medicine! It is actively working on your heart to heal it. I picture an infected wound that someone pours rubbing alcohol on; it stings terribly, but it kills the deadly bacteria allowing the wound to heal.

God wants to heal the heart of every person. He wants His Word to go forth being poured liberally on our hearts so that healing can begin. Some people refuse to expose their hearts to his healing words, but for those who receive them, healing will come.

Write out Psalm 147:3. *He heals the broken hearted and binds up their wounds*

3. **Sharper than any two-edged sword**
God's Word is alive and interacting with the needs of our hearts; it liberally pours itself on us to bring healing, and it cuts away and exposes the bacteria of sin in one decisive thrust.

4. **It penetrates even to dividing soul and spirit, joints and marrow.**
With supernatural ability, the Word of God is able to pierce our hearts and separate issues that we didn't even know existed. God's Word knows us better than we know ourselves.

5. **It judges the thoughts and attitudes of the heart.**
The first thing that I thought of was a polygraph test. We can't read minds, but God's Word can reach into our hearts and divide our thoughts from our attitudes. God never wonders what we are really thinking or the motivation for our actions. He knows, and He allows His word to penetrate deep into our hearts exposing the truth to us. It is the revelation of this truth that causes us to recognize who we really are and how desperately we need God.

I know that this lesson was a lot more lecture than actual homework for you, but before we finish, I would like you to write out Hebrews 4:13. *There is no creature hidden from His sight, but all things are naked and open to the eyes of Him to whom we must give an account*

Based on this verse, can you think of a reason that Satan would do almost anything to keep a soldier of the cross from using his sword? _____

One thought to ponder as we leave: Maybe one of the reasons that Satan flees when we resist him with the Word of God is that his heart is laid bare and he runs away to hide from the pain that God's Word causes him. Just a thought. *resist the devil and he will flee*

Psalm 119:93 I will never forget Your precepts, for You have given me life through them.

Dressed for the Business at Hand

Dress Check:

If, as you completed this lesson, the Word of God was penetrating your heart about an issue, take the time to listen to Him and let Him do a healing work in your heart right now. Dialogue with Him about what He has laid upon your heart.

_____
_____
_____
_____

Lesson 3

The Purpose of the Sword

For everyone who calls on the name of the Lord will be saved. Romans 10:13

We cannot begin to fathom or understand the ways of God, and that should make us happy because if we could understand Him, He wouldn't be a GREAT God. We don't ever want to minimize God; we don't want Him to fit into our limited minds. God has lovingly revealed glimpses of His glory, majesty, power, and holiness to us throughout His Word so that we can begin to understand just an inkling of who He is. We can be sure that whatever our minds have comprehended about God, He is all of that and then much more!

What did we learn that the sword of the spirit was according to Ephesians 6:17?
It's the Word of God

The Word revealed their God

Read Exodus 19:3-6; this is the covenant proposal that God offered to His chosen people. What did God say that this people would be to Him? *a kingdom of priests; a holy nation*

How did they respond to this proposal of relationship (vs. 7-8)? *All that the LORD has spoken we will do*

Read Exodus 19:9-25. How was God going to show himself to the people (vs. 9)? *in a thick cloud*

Who was He going to speak to? Why? *Moses*

Which verse is the fulfillment of this promise? _____

After God spoke to Moses in front of the entire assembly of people, He summoned Moses to the top of the mountain and He told Moses that he needed to warn the people again not to come up on the mountain. Moses told God that he had already told the people that they were not to come near or touch the Mountain. God commanded Moses to warn the people one more time that they should not touch the mountain of God or come near it.

What event was about to happen that might tempt the people to come up the mountain? _____

Write out Exodus 20:1. _And God spoke_

What are words that God spoke in Exodus 20:2-17? _the 10 Commandments relating to God and man_

I had never understood that God had spoken the 10 Commandments to the people from the top of that mountain, had you? I had always been taught that God had **only** written them on tablets of stone and that Moses came down and made them known to the people. Are you still wondering? Read Exodus 20:18-22 and Deuteronomy 4:10-13; 32-38. Believe me now? The Word of God, being spoken to this people, is what separated them from any other nation. God gave His words to His people so they could have life.

The first word in Deuteronomy 6:4 is the Hebrew word *Shema*; it means to hear. The people of God had **heard** God and His Word, and that is what convinced them that He was the LORD God.

God's words demanded respect
Numbers 15:30-31 gives us an example of the importance that God placed on obeying His words. A man was to be killed if he committed what sin (vs. 31)? _breaking God's Commandments_

To rebel against the Word of the LORD, was to invite judgment on one's life.

Obeying God's Word brought the reward of God's blessing
In Deuteronomy 32:44-47 as Moses concluded his teaching of the words of the LORD to the younger generation, what did he say that the words would be to the people if they followed them (vs. 47)? _you shall prolong the your days in the land_

To obey the things God said would bring the blessing of God.

God's words rejected
The Word of the LORD is delivered to people many times through leaders, judges, kings, prophets, and priests. Many people accepted His words and followed them, but often people rebelled against God's commands. As we near the end of the Old Testament period, God sent prophets to tell the people to repent, but what did the people do in Zechariah 7:8-12 when confronted with the Word of God? _they refused to heed to God's word_

Dressed for the Business at Hand

God's words withheld
God's people repeatedly refused to obey His words, so God stopped talking to them for a while. What kind of famine does God say He will send in Amos 8:11-12? _____

The book of Malachi is the last recorded word of God to His people in the Old Testament, and four-hundred years would pass before God would speak again to his people.

God's Word with us
Matthew 1:23 See, the virgin will become pregnant and give birth to a son, and they will name Him Immanuel, which is translated _____
Write out John 1:1. _____
_____
_____

In John 1:1, the Greek word *Logos* is used for the word *word*. It means thought or word. It is the expression of one's thoughts and being.

God Himself was revealed to us in the person of Jesus Christ. When Phillip asked Jesus to show him the Father, how did Jesus respond (John 14:8-10)? _____
_____

God had manifested His very presence among mankind to personally deliver His words of redemption and salvation. Some believed and followed Him, others mocked and ridiculed Him. They ultimately rejected his testimony and crucified Him. God's plan, however, was not defeated, for by the death of Jesus, the way had been made for all of mankind to know God and experience the indwelling of the Holy Spirit of God.

God's Word witnessed
We are called to be Christ's witnesses, to the uttermost parts of the Earth (Acts 1:8). We are to take the words of God that Christ spoke to this world and speak them to the generation in which we live.

The purpose of the sword is to reveal God. The Word of God always reveals God. Aren't you glad that someone brought the words of God to you so that you could see God?

There is an end to the timetable of life for mankind on Earth. Why do you think God has not returned to judge those who have rejected the testimony of His Word (II Peter 3:9). _____
_____
_____

I John 5:9-12 If we accept the testimony of men, God's testimony is greater, because it is God's testimony that He has given about His Son. ¹⁰ (The one who believes in the Son of God has this testimony within him. The one who does not believe God has made Him a liar, because he has not believed in the testimony God has given about His Son.) ¹¹ And this is the testimony: God has given us eternal life, and this life is in His Son. ¹² The one who has the Son has life. The one who doesn't have the Son of God does not have life.

When Christ comes in Revelation 19:11-16 to set up His Kingdom of righteousness upon Earth, and to judge the rebellion of those who have rejected Him, what is said to be coming out of His mouth (vs. 15)? _____

The words that He speaks will reveal God to all those who have rejected Him, and they will perish before Him. So great is their offense of having rejected His testimony (vs. 21).

We have been outfitted with the sword of the spirit to successfully complete the works that God has planned for us to do. As we hold forth the Word of God, we have His authority and power, and by it we reveal God to the world around us. Not everyone will accept His Word, but how will they believe unless they hear it?

Romans 10:13-15 For everyone who calls on the name of the Lord will be saved. But how can they call on Him they have not believed in? And how can they believe without hearing about Him? And how can they hear without a preacher? ¹⁵ And how can they preach unless they are sent? As it is written: How beautiful are the feet of those who announce the gospel of good things!

Dress Check:

How important are the words of the Lord to you? _____
_____

Write a prayer to God thanking Him that someone came and shared His words with you so that God was revealed to you and you were saved from your sin. _____
_____
_____
_____

Dressed for the Business at Hand

Lesson 4

Possessing the Sword

And whatever you do, in word or in deed, do everything in the name of the Lord Jesus, giving thanks to God the Father through Him. Colossians 3:17

In our first week of study we examined the importance of the Word of God in our lives. We learned that it was crucial to know God's Word in order for it to guide us in our walk. Knowing the truth of God's Word ensures that we won't be deceived by the enemy's lies. The defensive aspect of the Belt of Truth is that we are applying the power of God's Word to our own lives. The offensive quality of the sword is that we take what we know is truth in our lives, and we carefully apply it to other people's lives, revealing God to them.

Today's lesson will point out some evidences of the sword being used; tomorrow we will see evidence of a sword in its sheath.

God's covenant with His people in the Old Testament was a written code of laws. Following the rules and laws were evidence that you were following Jehovah God. In the New Testament (which actually means New Covenant), God's ministry in people's lives changed from the outward signs of the law to an inward work of renewing people's hearts.

Read Hebrews 8:8-13. What will be written upon the minds and the hearts of the people? _____

How does that occur?

Write out John 14:16. _____
_____

Where will this Spirit of truth live? _____

What will he do for us in John 14:26? _____

Whose words will the Spirit be speaking to us (John 16:13)? _____

What will be the result?

Read Matthew 12:33-37. If the Spirit of God has made a life good, what will be the evidence of this change (v33)? _____

According to verse 34, what comes out of our mouths? _____

Who will be affected?

Read Colossians 3:16. As the Word of Christ dwells in us richly (with great abundance), what activities will result? _____
_____
_____

I like to call this "splashing." I have some friends who splash God all over me when we talk. Their hearts are so full of God that He spills over on everyone who comes near them. Do you know anyone like this? Write the names of people who splash God on you whenever you talk with them. _____
_____

Maybe you have a lot of names, and I surely hope that you do, but I wish my list was longer. I know a lot of Christians, but sometimes their conversations are negative, gossipy, and empty. The circle of friends that I have who speak with excellence from their hearts is much smaller. I believe that small number of splashers saddens the heart of God. Each one of us, as His beloved bride, should be so passionately in love with Him that we are eager to spend time in His Word getting to know Him, and then as we learn of Him, we won't be able to keep our mouths quiet and we will become splashers!

What should be coming out of our mouths according to Ephesians 5:19-20? _____
_____

It doesn't sound as if using our swords is optional, we have been blessed to have the Spirit of God in our hearts. He is teaching us God's Word, and we should be sharing what we have learned with others.

Why do we wield our swords?

In II Timothy 3:16, what functions does God's Word have? _____
_____

It changes lives. The living, active, sharp, penetrating sword of God's Word is useful to change the lives of people around us. As we complete the works God has planned for us, the sword of the Spirit and the Word of God will change people's lives.

When do we raise our swords?

Read Matthew 12:36-37. How many of our words will we have to give an account for when we stand in front of God? _____

Dressed for the Business at Hand

Write out I Peter 4:11a. _____
_____

We have been called to be witnesses for Jesus Christ with our lives. The Spirit of God has been placed within us to teach us all things. So when we speak, we need to be very careful to represent Him well by raising our swords to honor Him.

Colossians 3:17 And whatever you do, in word or in deed, do everything in the name of the Lord Jesus, giving thanks to God the Father through Him.

Dress Check:

Was the mirror of God's word a reflection of how you speak? _____ If not, what can you do to change what people hear as they spend time with you?
_____
_____
_____
_____
_____
_____
_____
_____
_____
_____
_____
_____
_____

The Word of God is a sword. It has the power to bring healing to the hearts of mankind by cutting out the decay of sin. However, we are told in Ephesians 4:15 to speak the truth in love. Be careful swinging your sword!

Lesson 5

Swordless

It is such a blessing to be around someone who is speaking the Word of God wisely. There are times when our spirits are encouraged and lifted, and there are times when we are rebuked and confronted, but each type of encounter is for our benefit. God's Word always has a harvest.

Read Isaiah 55:10-11. Write out verse 11. _____
_____

We need both the sun and the rain to accomplish the harvest of righteousness that God is planting in our hearts through His Word.

We talked yesterday about the fruit that would be evident in the life of a believer who is holding the sword of the Spirit in his hands. We read Scripture that told us that psalms, hymns, spiritual songs and thanksgiving should regularly be coming out our mouths; only words that build others up and minister the grace of God should be escaping past our lips.

I forewarned you that today's lesson would reveal symptoms found in the life of a believer whose sword was sheathed. If you remember back to our helmet of salvation lessons, the primary reason believers don't pick up the sword and use it is because their hands are already full. They are carrying around with them the corpse of their old nature, afraid to lay it down and embrace the new life of Christ. When we carry around our old natures, our priority becomes "me, my, and I."

In our lesson yesterday, I mentioned that I had some Christian friends who spewed gossip or criticism when they spoke. A decade ago that described me. I did not let the Word of Christ dwell in me richly, I was not fully clothed in the armor of God; I was mired down in sin, preoccupied with 'me, myself and I,' and out of the abundance of that self-centered heart, I spoke.

I didn't spend much time reading God's Word or maybe I would have seen my reflection in the many passages that describe how Christians are **not** to live. My refusal to wear the helmet of salvation and my preoccupation with my own needs caused me to say many unkind, unnecessary things. I am so thankful that God looked down upon my sorry life and said, "Jodie, you are content to eat the crumbs off the floor, but I have promised that you could eat **at** my banquet table." God very directly led me to do some in-depth Bible studies and His Word has truly become life to me. I have eaten from the table and I don't ever want to go back to the floor!

Dressed for the Business at Hand

When a soldier's sword is sheathed and their hands are carrying the corpse of the old nature, what type of fruit will come from their mouth? Read Ephesians 4:20-32. List the sins mentioned in this passage that are associated with our old natures. _____
_____
_____

As you look at that list, underline the sins mentioned that are related to the mouth.

Write out the specific sins of the mouth mentioned in Ephesians 5:1-11. _____
_____
_____

Because we have been raised with Christ in heavenly places, Colossians 3:2 says that we are to set our minds on heavenly things. Read verses 7-10 and list the sins that will be committed by a person whose mind is not set on Christ. _____
_____

These epistles were written to Christian churches, and these admonitions were being given to Christian believers. The rebuke is that these sins represent the way our old nature speaks, but it should not be the way a child of God speaks.

A believer who is swordless in battle is still holding onto his pride and to his own priority agenda—the corpse of his old nature. This swordless believer will still make it to heaven; his salvation is secure. But instead of having shared the truth with others and setting many free, he will arrive in heaven empty handed because all corpses are checked at heaven's gate.

Dress Check:

Maybe after today's lesson you recognized yourself in some of the Scriptures that describe a swordless life. Maybe you need to quiet your heart before God and ask His forgiveness. Ask, too, for the courage to place the helmet of salvation upon your head. _____
_____
_____
_____

It is never too late to be a soldier of the cross. Unsheathe your sword and in His authority and power go and make disciples of all nations!

Ladies, today my heart has been tendered by the thought of arriving at heaven's gate and having Jesus say to me, "I had so many things planned for you to do for me, but because you wouldn't trust me enough to wear the helmet of salvation, you never got to use the sword of my Word to accomplish those tasks."

I want to lay aside all fear of my own needs and desires and press ahead for the cause of Jesus Christ.

I have an 8x10 picture frame on my wall with the following declaration. The copy that I have says that it was written by an African pastor and that he tacked to his wall. I think that your heart will identify with this man's desire, as did mine.

My Commitment as a Christian

I'm part of the fellowship of the unashamed. I have Holy Spirit Power. The die has been cast. I have stepped over the line. The decision has been made. I'm a disciple of His. I won't look back, let up, slow down, back away or be still.

My past is redeemed, my present makes sense, and my future is secure. I'm finished and done with low living, sight-walking, small planning, smooth knees, colorless dreams, tamed visions, mundane talking, cheap living and dwarfed goals.

I no longer need preeminence, pleasure, possessions, prosperity, position, promotions, plaudits or popularity. I don't have to be right, first, tops, recognized, praised, regarded or rewarded. I now live by faith, lean on His presence, walk by patience, lift by prayer and labor by power.

My face is set, my pace is fast, my goal is heaven, my road is narrow, my way rough, my companions few, my Guide reliable, my mission clear. I cannot be bought, compromised, detoured, lured away, turned back, deluded or delayed. I will not flinch in the face of sacrifice, hesitate in the presence of the adversary, negotiate at the table of the enemy, ponder at the pool of popularity or meander in the maze of mediocrity.

I won't give up, shut up, let up, until I have stayed up, stored up, prayed up, paid up, preached up for the cause of Christ. I am a disciple of Jesus. I must go till He comes, give till I drop, preach till all know and work till He stops me. And when He comes for His own, He will have no problem recognizing me, my banner will be clear.

Dressed for the Business at Hand

Unsheathed

We have been given the Sword of the Spirit, the words of life! I was teaching this last lesson on the armor of God to a sweet group of ladies at my church, and as it would happen, this particular lesson would be their last Bible study session for the year. Before I got up to teach, they rehearsed all of the lessons they had studied throughout the year and then they shared prayer requests and spent some time in prayer.

As I listened to the heart-wrenching prayer requests: illnesses, lost jobs, loneliness, rebellious children, strained relationships, foreclosures etc. etc. etc., my heart ached and stomach was in knots. These were all serious situations, and each request was shared out of personal pain and a desire to survive and honor God in the midst of the situation.

My heart was burdened with their pain, but when I stood to speak and bring this lesson on the sword, the words of life, the Spirit of God spoke to my heart and my lesson on the words of life went a little like this:

> I celebrate with you the conclusion of another year of Bible study. I am so happy that you have a desire to know God and to know His Word, to hide His Word in your heart so that you might not sin against Him. I want you to know that your desire and commitment to come each week is praiseworthy. I am happy for you and you encourage me, but I feel like I cannot end this Bible study series and your year of studying the Bible without sharing a bit of a warning that I find in Scripture.
>
> If you open your Bible and read II Timothy 3:1-9, you will find a shocking description of the way people will be in the last days. People are described as: lovers of self, lovers of money, boastful, proud, blasphemers, disobedient to parents, ungrateful, unholy, unloving, irreconcilable, slanders, without self-control, brutal, without love for what is good, traitors, reckless, conceited, lovers of pleasure rather than God, acting like they have religion but really not knowing God.
>
> The deep and sorrowful situations that we just petitioned our holy God for help with are products of sinful people who live in a sinful world. There is hurt, pain, and destruction in this broken world. Broken people hurt other people; we are all in desperate need of God and His life-giving words that heal and bring hope.
>
> Verses six and seven add another description of what people will be like in the last days and it specifically describes women. The descriptors are that women are idle, burdened down with sin, being led by a variety of passions, and always learning but never being able to acknowledge the truth.
>
> That is the verse in this passage of Scripture that scares me to death. It is like a huge warning to me because it says in the last days there will be women who are always

learning but never acknowledging the truth! That is scary. Can we open this book, learn from it, and not be changed? Yes, we can. We can be hearers of God's Word but not doers. We can look into the mirror of God's Word see what needs to be changed and walk away changing nothing.

In the past 15-20 years, there has been an explosion of Bible studies among women in our country. As women we have had the privilege of studying God's Word with some of the best Bible teachers (both men and women) our generation has ever known. I have been involved in multiple Bible studies every year for at least 25 years and I am sure that many of you have been as well. But the question begs to be asked and it must be answered honestly: Are we different because we have spent time studying God's Word? Are we better wives? Are we committed to our husbands? Have we kept our marriage vows and been a helpmeet to him? Are we better parents? Do we parent our children with the primary focus of raising up a godly generation? Do we really desire that above all our children know God and love Him? Do we pray that they will hate sin and not be entrapped by the deceptions of the world? What kind of friends are we? Are we loyal, like God is loyal – faithful and loving? What kind of employers or employees are we? Do others see God when they see us? When we speak are others refreshed and encouraged by our words?

If we have heard God's Words and obeyed them, then the answer will be a resounding "Yes!" God's words bring life and light! They bring peace, joy, healing, and hope! God's words guide our steps and they correct us when we go astray! He disciplines those whom He loves as dearly beloved children. God's words in our hearts keep us from being deceived and pursuing the things of the world! He satisfies our souls! He is absolutely everything He has claimed to be, and we can trust Him, walking in faith, dying to self for the pleasure of God Himself living through us! Amazing God!

If, unfortunately, we have had to answer "no" to these questions, then unfortunately we may be like the women in these verses in II Timothy 3, always learning but never acknowledging the truth. May it not be true of me; may it not be true of you.

However difficult it is for us to hear this right now, all of those heart-rending prayer requests that we just laid at His feet, He knows about them and in His kind and sovereign will, He has authorized them. These difficulties may be the way that He chooses to reveal Himself to us – like a "ghost" on the water, drawing near to us in our storm. He wants us to know Him and the power of His resurrection; He wants to show up big in our lives and do a saving work. He also has works prepared for us to do in this world so that others will see Him through us. We may not want the hardship and we may cry out because of it, but know that He hears you and that He has drawn near to you. Do not fight against Him; you can trust Him. Be still and let Him work through you and your situation. His presence and power shine through the darkest of nights, as bright as a pillar of fire guiding the lost to Himself!

When we speak God's life-giving words to those around us, we are showing broken people what God is like and we can speak words that bring healing and forgiveness, words that bring life and light to them.

You have spent this last year studying God's Word, not for the shallow, empty purpose of gaining head knowledge, but so that your heart has been prepared to let Jesus live through you! I know that your situations are still painful—Sin hurts us deeply and it hurts the ones that we love, but I pray that you will look at your situation a little differently today, knowing that God is standing near to you, strengthening you and desiring for you to let Him live through you by sharing His life-giving words with others.

In a nutshell that is the message that I shared with those sweet ladies as they faced such difficult situations in life. I am guessing that if I could sit down with you today over a cup of coffee, I would find that you have some storms in your life too, things that seem unfair and painful. I may not be able to answer your *why*, but I can tell you about the *who*. I know that when we are wearing the armor of God we walk confidently with Him as He leads us. We have our eyes and our hearts set on Him, we are obedient to His call, and we are sheltered by faith. We die to ourselves, and yet in doing so, we know the fullness of Christ living in us!

When we enter a storm fully protected by the armor of God, we are protected from the enemy's attempt to destroy us in the storm! We are safe behind our shield. It doesn't mean the storm goes away, but we face it with our hand tucked in the hand of God and we do not fear. When life's journey finally ends for us and we safely cross the finish line of heaven, we will celebrate with an excited hand pump over our heads. God wants to strengthen us with His power so that we finish well!

We need to handle the sword carefully. We have already mentioned how painful the storms of life can be. Pain does funny things to people; it can soften their hearts or make them as hard as stone. We have the privilege of speaking God's life giving words to hurting, broken people, people who may not even know they are trapped in sin's snare, separated from God. So when we share God's life giving words, we need to speak wisdom with love. Jesus told His disciples that love would authenticate their message (John 13:34-35). Beating people up with the club of God's Word discredits the voice of God. That kind of "truth" doesn't bring life to people. Jesus did not shame the woman at the well; clearly she was living an immoral lifestyle, but privately and compassionately Jesus spoke truth over her life, and she was drawn to the Giver of life.

The devil doesn't want God's truth to be known because it brings wisdom, life, peace, and joy. Satan doesn't want you to handle the sword of the Spirit with skill and compassion, but ladies, we need to unsheathe our swords and when God opens a door for us to speak truth into a life, we need to speak.

Hebrews 4:12 For the word of God is living and effective and sharper than any double-edged sword, penetrating as far as the separation of soul and spirit, joints and marrow. It is able to judge the ideas and thoughts of the heart.

God's Word performs the surgery, and as the sin is removed God's Spirit comes and dwells within that repentant heart, bringing life. **II Corinthians 5:17 Therefore, if anyone is in Christ, he is a new creation; old things have passed away, and look, new things have come**

Dressed for the Business at Hand

The sword of the Spirit brings life to people who bow their knees and confess the Lord Jesus; however, there is a day coming when it will lay bare the hearts of the unrepentant and strike them down.

Revelation 19:11-16 Then I saw heaven opened, and there was a white horse. Its rider is called Faithful and True, and He judges and makes war in righteousness. ¹² His eyes were like a fiery flame, and many crowns were on His head. He had a name written that no one knows except Himself. ¹³ He wore a robe stained with blood, and His name is the Word of God. ¹⁴ The armies that were in heaven followed Him on white horses, wearing pure white linen. ¹⁵ A sharp sword came from His mouth, so that He might strike the nations with it. He will shepherd them with an iron scepter. He will also trample the winepress of the fierce anger of God, the Almighty. ¹⁶ And He has a name written on His robe and on His thigh: KING OF KINGS AND LORD OF LORDS. And then in verse 21 **the rest were killed with the sword that came from the mouth of the rider on the horse, and all the birds were filled with their flesh.**

The very words of God which today bring life to the deadened souls of mankind will one day pierce their hearts and seal their eternal fate.

Until God takes us home or sends Jesus to bring us up to heaven, let us walk fully protected in this broken world, and with **unsheathed** swords, let us share the words of life.

*If you have children you may wish to read the lesson on the sword of the Spirit in *The Armored Baton* (page 161).

The Armored Baton

Supplemental Resource for Parents
Jodie Sewall

The Armored Baton

Supplemental Resource for Parents

A Study of the Spiritual Armor of God

2012

Sewall Publishing

All Rights Reserved

Printed in the United States of America

Unless otherwise noted, all Scripture quotations are taken from the Holman Christian Standard Bible® Copyright © 1999, 2000, 2002, 2003 by Holman Bible Publishers. Used by permission. Holman Christian Standard Bible®, Holman CSB®, and HCSB® are federally registered trademarks of Holman Bible Publishers.

THE HOLY BIBLE, NEW INTERNATIONAL VERSION®, NIV® Copyright © 1973, 1978, 1984, 2011 by Biblica, Inc.™ Used by permission. All rights reserved worldwide.

The Privilege & the Responsibility

From the moment we held that tiny baby bundled tightly in the hospital blanket and looked into those trusting eyes, we began a love affair of the heart with our child.

Psalm 127 tells us that children are a heritage from the Lord and that a man is blessed to have his quiver full of them!

God determined that you are ready for his greatest assignment—to raise up a godly generation.

Malachi 2:15. . And what does the One seek? A godly offspring.
Psalm 127:3 . . . Sons is indeed a heritage from the LORD, children, a reward

This assignment from God is both exciting and daunting; it requires a 24/7 commitment for about twenty years and an on-call status for life. It isn't easy, but we know that the greatest reward will be watching our children walk with God. That is worth all the sacrifice along the way.

3 John 4 I have no greater joy than this: to hear that my children are walking in the truth.

In regards to the spiritual education of our children, the Bible gives us some clear examples, directives, and instructions:

- **Repeat them to your children. Talk about them when you sit in your house and when you walk along the road, when you lie down and when you get up.** Deuteronomy 6:7
- **Imprint these words of mine on your hearts and minds . . . Teach them to your children, talking about them when you sit in your house and when you walk along the road, when you lie down and when you get up.** Deuteronomy 11:18-19
- **. . . I will declare wise sayings; I will speak mysteries from the past— ³ things we have heard and known and that our fathers have passed down to us. ⁴ We must not hide them from their children, but must tell a future generation the praises of the LORD, His might, and the wonderful works He has performed.** Psalm 78:2-4
- **Teach a youth about the way he should go; even when he is old he will not depart from it.** Proverbs 22:6
- **She opens her mouth with wisdom and loving instruction is on her tongue. ²⁷ She watches over the activities of her household and is never idle. ²⁸ Her sons rise up and call her blessed. Her husband also praises her.** Proverbs 31:26-28
- **Fathers, don't stir up anger in your children, but bring them up in the training and instruction of the Lord.** Ephesians 6:4

The Armored Baton

> o . . . and you know that from childhood you have known the sacred Scriptures. . .
> II Timothy 3:15

There are many other Scriptures that would attest to this awesome responsibility and privilege, but we can clearly see from these that we have a personal responsibility in raising godly children.

The standard is high because it is God's standard. He has set the bar high because He desires godly offspring.

Why is it seemingly hard to attain this goal? Why do we hear so often in student testimonies that they were raised in Christian homes, but they lived a double life, one life in front of their parents, pretending to follow God, and another life totally depraved when they were with their friends?

I seem to hear that type of testimony more often than I hear, "I was raised in a Christian home and I grew to love God more and more and my heart's desire is to know him better." Is there any hope to raise our children in such a way? I think so.

[Margin note: Jer. 17:9 - The heart is deceitful above all things And desperately wicked; Who can know it? / Mt. 15:19]

What is the stumbling block in our families? What happens that causes our kids' hearts to grow lukewarm or cold to the things of God? I believe that Satan gains a foothold of deceit in their lives, and once his foot is in, he wiggles himself in more and more, eventually completely deceiving the kids. Satan is then successful in hindering the plan of God to raise a godly generation who in turn has the great task of raising the next generation!

If you knew there was a wild man loose in the neighborhood and that he was known to kill and destroy, would you let your kids ride their bikes alone? I am sure you would ride with your kids, pointing out potential hiding spots, and you would be warning and preparing them for possible encounters. You would remind them daily to be on the lookout and to be prepared. Life would most assuredly be lived at a heightened level.

Do you know what the enemy of our families looks like? Do you know how he operates?
- He deceives & corrupts (2 Cor. 11:3).
- He destroys people (I Peter 5:8).
- He lies (John 8:44).
- He blasphemes God (Rev. 13:6).
- He tempts (Matt. 4:3).
- He kills (John 8:44).
- He accuses (Rev. 12:10).
- He rules this earthly kingdom (Eph. 2:2).
- He disguises himself (2 Cor. 11:14).

Oh my! That is what the enemy of our families looks like!

I recently watched a mother turtle digging a hole to lay her eggs. When the mama turtle began to lay her eggs in the hole, a large crow landed on the ground near her and began plucking the eggs away before the mother turtle even had a chance to bury them. I was angry at the audacity of the crow and I marched out and stood guard over the turtle until she was finished laying and burying her eggs, then I carefully concealed the area to protect it from the horrible, terrorizing crow.

Isn't that crow just like Satan? Satan hates! He is full of hate and destruction! He doesn't care the slightest bit about our children. He doesn't feel sympathy because they are young, vulnerable, inexperienced, or cute. He wants to destroy them. We need to be on guard against him.

We don't need to fear the devil; we are more than conquerors through Jesus Christ, and nothing shall be able to separate us from the love of God (Rom. 8:37). We don't have to be afraid, but we certainly need to be aware of him and his desire to destroy our families. If we forget about him, we are apt to become complacent and fail to teach, train, and warn our children, and they may become his next victim

So how do we raise a godly generation in the midst of spiritual warfare? Read Ephesians 6:10-18.

God has provided the protection that we need to be safe from the deception of the devil. When we dress ourselves in the armor of God and instruct our children in God's protection, we will pass our baton of faith safely to the next generation, protected by the armor of God.

We live in the world, but we don't want the world to live in us. Let's walk beside each other for a few weeks, studying God's Word and hopefully by the time we part company we will each be fully dressed in the armor of God and equipped to teach our children about God's awesome protection for them.

I received this article as an e-mail once and I have seen it posted on the internet. It is written by Alvin Reid and it is a sobering look at the devil and his work.

Are we too busy?
Satan called a worldwide convention of demons. In his opening address he said, "We can't keep Christians from going to church. We can't keep them from reading their Bibles and knowing the truth. We can't even keep them from forming an intimate relationship with their SAVIOR. Once they gain that connection with JESUS, our power over them is broken. So let them go to their churches; let them have their covered dish dinners, BUT steal their time, so they don't have time to develop a relationship

The Armored Baton

with JESUS CHRIST. This is what I want you to do," said the devil: "Distract them from gaining hold of their SAVIOR and maintaining that vital connection throughout their day!"
"How shall we do this?" his demons shouted.

"Keep them busy in the non-essentials of life and invent innumerable schemes to occupy their minds," he answered. "Tempt them to spend, spend, spend, and borrow, borrow, borrow. Persuade the wives to go to work for long hours and the husbands to work 6-7 days each week, 10-12 hours a day, so they can afford their empty lifestyles. Keep them from spending time with their children. As their families fragment, soon, their homes will offer no escape from the pressures of work!

Over-stimulate their minds so that they cannot hear that still, small voice. Entice them to play the radio or I-Pod whenever they drive, to keep the TV, DVDs, CDs and their PCs going constantly in their home and see to it that every store and restaurant in the world plays non-biblical music constantly. This will jam their minds and break that union with CHRIST.

But even that isn't enough; fill the coffee tables with magazines and newspapers. Pound their minds with the news 24 hours a day. Invade their driving moments with billboards. Flood their mailboxes with junk mail, mail order catalogs, sweepstakes, and every kind of newsletter and promotional offering free products, services and false hopes.

Keep skinny, beautiful models on the magazines and TV so their husbands will believe that outward beauty is what's important, and they'll become dissatisfied with their wives. Keep the wives too tired to love their husbands at night. Give them headaches too! If they don't give their husbands the love they need, they will begin to look elsewhere. That will fragment their families quickly!

Give them Santa Claus to distract them from teaching their children the real meaning of Christmas. Give them an Easter bunny so they won't talk about HIS resurrection and power over sin and death.

Even in their recreation, let them be excessive. Have them return from their recreation exhausted. Keep them too busy to go out in nature and reflect on GOD'S creation. Send them to amusement parks, sporting events, plays, concerts, and movies instead. Keep them busy, busy, busy!

And when they meet for spiritual fellowship have them leave with troubled consciences. Crowd their lives with so many good causes they have no time to seek power from JESUS. Soon they will be working in their own strength, sacrificing their health and family for the good of the cause.

It will work! It will work!"

It was quite a plan! The demons went eagerly to their assignments causing Christians everywhere to get busier and more rushed, going here and there, having little time for their GOD or their families.

Ladies, let's commit that we will not become distracted in our goal of raising a godly family. Let's lift up our eyes and focus on things above and be busy about training up a generation of children who love the Lord and know Him.

The Belt of Truth

God's Word Can Be Trusted – the Belt of Truth

In our study on the belt of truth, we talked about the importance of God's Word as a filter to our minds. His Word, the truth, protects us from the deceptive lies the enemy wants us to believe to keep us from fulfilling the works that God has ordained for us to do.

Some of the tasks or works that God has for us to do in our lifetime are unknown to us; He is still preparing us for those tasks, but if we have children, we can be certain that He has entrusted us with a task that is near and dear to His heart, the task of raising up a godly generation!

As parents our primary task for the years that our children are in our homes is to mold, shape, and train our children's lives. The task is awesome and one that we cannot take lightly or relegate to other people.

We have briefly talked about our enemy, the devil, who prowls looking for people to devour. He is ruthless and determined to stop the works of God from being done. He hates it when people accept Christ as their Savior. He hates it when they mature as believers and then lead others to Christ. He will pull out all stops to hinder that work.

We talked about the belt of truth and the necessity of being in God's Word daily. We need it to filter out all the lies that we hear during the day, so that as we make decisions during the day, we can be confident that we are following God, accomplishing the work that He has for us to do.

When you think about how easy it is for us as grown women to become distracted from the work of God and how easy it is to be deceived into believing that we are simply too busy to spend time in God's Word, just think how easy it would be for Satan to distract our children and to cause them to doubt God's Word and the importance of God's Word in their lives.

Let's think about what types of things we can do to ensure that as we teach and train our children that we are instilling in them the confidence that God's Word is true and that it can be trusted in every area of their lives.

- Model what you teach.
    - As you teach them Biblical truths of how God desires us to live (kindness, loving, joyful, long-suffering, faithful, peacefully, patiently, gently and self-controlled), be sure that you practice what you preach. If we do this, our

The Armored Baton

children will attribute great value to the truths of God's Word. On the flip-side, if we teach them one thing but live a hypocritical life in front of them, they will place little esteem on God's words.

- Take time to teach your children Bible accounts.
  - Children love to hear their parents tell them stories, but be sure as you are telling them "stories" from God's Word that you tell them that these are true accounts and not just make-believe stories. Don't leave the Bible teaching to your child's Sunday school teacher; teaching is both our privilege and responsibility as parents.

- Encourage your children to memorize Scripture.
  - Pick Scripture that will be especially meaningful to them and applicable to their lives. If they are fearful about something, find a Scripture that reinforces that God is near them and with them. Whatever the situations your children are in, teach them a verse that will encourage them to make God-honoring decisions.

- Teach them the value of having a daily time with God.
  - Talk to your children about things that God has been teaching you in your time of Bible reading and prayer. Plan a time for your children to read the Bible and spend time with God. Word of Life Fellowship Inc. has wonderful resources available for families who want to share in a Quiet Time each day with God. www.wol.org

- As life happens around you, teach them the relevance of God's Word by talking about God's involvement in the affairs of men and the fulfillment of prophecy in the last days. Demonstrate to your children that God and His Word are relevant in their lives everyday, not just on Sunday. If your child is in a public school system, show them from the Bible that God created the world and that evolution is a world religion and not fact. God is involved in our lives every day, so let's make sure that our children grow up knowing that He is and that His Word can be trusted.

This first piece of armor is tremendously valuable to have in place in our children's lives. It is also one that we can inadvertently undermine with our inconsistency or an uninvolved approach. Raising children who highly esteem God and His Word will not happen by accident; it will take parents who purposefully make the effort to model and teach their value.

Help you children to gird up their minds with God's Word so they can filter the information they receive through His Word and make wise decisions about living a life that pleases God.

Train up a child in the way he should go; and when he is old he will not depart from it.

Teach a youth about the way he should go; even when he is old he will not depart from it.
Proverbs 22:6

Foolishness is bound up in the heart of a child, but the rod of correction will drive it far from him. Prov 22:15

Do not withhold correction from a child for if you beat him (spank) w/a rod, he will not die. Prov. 23:13

He who spares his rod hates his son, But he who loves (spanks) him disciplines him promptly. Prov. 13:24

The Breastplate of Righteousness

God is All-Sufficient

In our study of the breastplate of righteousness, we learned the importance of setting our hearts on things above. As the Bride of Christ, we are in a love relationship with the very One who made our redemption possible. He loved us and gave Himself for us, cleansing us by covering us with His own righteousness; our hearts belong to him. He is all-sufficient for us and He promises that He came that we might have life and have it to the full.

Our enemy, the devil, does not want you or your children to believe that. He doesn't want us to discover that true contentment, peace, and joy can only be found in Jesus, so he tries to convince us that we need other things to be happy and content and satisfied in this world. If we believe his lie, we will embrace false gods and abandon our first love with Jesus Christ. We become tainted brides who share what belongs to Jesus, our hearts, with the enemy.

It is important that we teach our children that having money, power, fame or things will never bring them satisfaction. The TV and most other forms of media tell them otherwise. They will hear repeatedly that they **need (fill in the blank)** to be happy. The enemy wants them to think they need the latest, greatest invention or game or car or thing. If our children buy into the lies, they will live on a perpetual search which always leads away from God.

How can we ensure that we teach our kids that what they see and hear everyday is simply not the answer to their desires of contentment and satisfaction? Here are a few suggestions for your consideration.

- Model a grateful spirit towards God.
    - Give thanks to God everyday for the food that He has provided.
    - Give thanks to God for the safety He gives as you travel to and from your daily activities.
    - Give thanks for your health and the health of your friends.
    - Give thanks for God's provision of a home to live in and a vehicle to drive.
    - Recognize God's hand of provision in any special gifts that come your way.

    As we thank God often for the ways that He provides for us as a family, our children begin to connect that God is the source of all the blessings in our lives. Be vigilant against complaining spirits, both yours as the parents and your children. Teach that a complaining spirit means that the complainer is saying they could do a better job than God is doing.
- Model contentment.
    - Show your children that you don't have to run and buy a new car on credit just because there are newer or cooler models out now. Drive your car until God makes a way for you to purchase a newer one or until the one that you have

The Armored Baton

simply cannot meet your needs anymore. Model a grateful spirit for what God has given you.
- This same principle is true in whatever new-fangled thing it is that comes out—new video games, new computers, new cell-phones, new movie, etc. If you live your life, "needing" every new thing that comes out, you will be sabotaging your efforts to communicate to your children that God is sufficient for your needs. Do not believe the lie that you cannot be happy unless you have God + (fill in the blank).
- Model an open-hand mentality to the things of this world.
    - Be willing to share your possessions with people who are in need.
    - Show your children I John 2:15-16, James 4, and other Scriptures about those who love the world and the things of the world. Teach them that loving God is of primary importance.
    - Relax about things that get broken or lost; demonstrate forgiveness and love to people. People are always more important than things—ALL things.
- Teach your children Scriptures about contentment.
    - Using the "I Am's" of Christ found in the gospel of John, show them how Jesus has promised to meet their deepest soul needs.
    - Teach them how to set their hearts affections on things above.

As you live your lives with an open-hand mentality, thankful for all that God has given you and with a willingness to share those blessings with others, you will be teaching your children that heart contentment does not come from the false-gods (things) in this world, but rather from knowing God, loving Him, and serving Him. That is where the true treasure is found. He is

Matthew 6:21 For where your treasure is, there your heart will be also.

God disciplines those whom He loves.

Teaching our children the importance of obedience seems like something that all parents understand; however, in the age we live obedience is not as clearly understood and taught has it has been in times past. Parents today often prefer to demonstrate mercy, patience, and long-suffering towards their children often to the exclusion of obedience and consequences.

Certainly there is a place within our training of our children to offer mercy, patience, and long-suffering, but it should always partner with discipline.

God has given parents the responsibility of training up a godly generation. Children left to their own devices will grow up with proud, self-centered, deceptive hearts. That is the very nature of sin and our sin nature. As we begin to teach and train our young children, we are introducing them to the idea that there is another way to live, a way that honors other people and that respects them and serves them. We do not need to wait until our children have accepted Christ as their Savior to introduce them to the way that God created man to live.

Training someone to think or act contrary to their natural desires takes time and repeated effort. It will demand the parents' focused attention and their sincere desire for what is best for the child.

Hebrews 12:5-11 teaches us that God the Father disciplines his children because He loves them and desires what is best for them. Discipline does not seem pleasant at the moment but it is working out a future blessing.

One important factor in teaching our children to obey us, their parents, is that we are setting the groundwork for their response to God. If children grow up with disrespectful, rebellious, and un-submissive spirits toward their parents, they will in all likelihood demonstrate that same independent and rebellious attitude toward God.

So what are some things can we do as parents that will help to shape the child's will into being obedient and respectful?
- Speak kindly and respectfully to your child. Yelling and screaming at them does not accomplish training in righteousness (James 1:20). This may be especially difficult for some parents as yelling may be the way they remember being disciplined. Break the cycle. Purpose in your heart to give dignity to your children. Even if they have been disobedient, they can expect to be treated with dignity.
- Be clear in your expectations.

Your Feet Sandaled with Readiness for the Gospel of Peace

- Make sure that children understand what you are asking them to do. Disobedience can sometimes happen unintentionally as a result of unclear expectations.
- Expect the child to obey your directions.
    - If you have looked them in the eye and asked them to do something and you know they understood your request, expect that they will be obedient. If they are not obedient, do not give them repeated chances to obey. That is really training our children to be "third-responders" instead of being "first-responders."
    - Be consistent. Obedience is the right response and should be expected at all times. If you only demand obedience on days when you are feeling grouchy and don't feel like dealing with their childishness but let them get away with everything on days when you are feeling happy and good, you will be raising a child who obeys only when they feel like it.
- Use Scripture verses that expose the nature of their disobedience.
    - If the child has refused to obey a specific request, show them verses about a rebellious spirit.
    - If the child has been unkind to someone, show them verses that teach that we need to be kind and respectful towards others.
    - Have your child sit in their room or on the couch or on the bottom of the stairs until you have had the opportunity to pray and ask God to show you what the sin issue really is and to help you find Scripture to teach the child.
- Demonstrate love to your child.
    - The purpose of discipline is to train your child. It is not to punish them or to make them feel unloved or unaccepted in your family. The purpose is to bring about a change in their heart that will help train them to be obedient in the future.
    - Hug your child and pray with them after you correct them. Make sure they know that you talk to God about their behavior and that their behavior is important to God.
- Give them examples of how you are being obedient to God.
    - Sometimes when you discipline, remind your child that you have a responsibility to obey God also. God has instructed parents to discipline their children, so when they sin, you must obey God and discipline them.
    - Letting your child know that you have to obey laws, rules, and authorities will help them to understand that obedience is something they will need to practice their whole life.
- Be committed for the long-haul.
    - Training takes time and commitment. Don't give up because your children don't seem to get it. As adults we are still learning and we get disciplined by God; so never, never, never give up teaching and disciplining your children. It will come!

Feet Fitted with Readiness

Approach your child-training years as a marathon: There will be times that seem easy and times that seem impossible; but push your way through and in the end, you will have trained up your children in the way that they should go, and when they are old – they will still be living that way!

Teach your children the importance of the having feet that are fitted for readiness!

The Armored Baton

Shield of Faith

God leads me and I follow.

Teaching our children the value of faith can seem challenging on some days and easy on others.

It can be easy to teach faith because children are naturally trusting. They believe what we tell them because they trust our word. Sharing the gospel with them is precious and sweet because their hearts are open and they want to accept Jesus and His gift of salvation. They easily recognize their sin and they eagerly embrace forgiveness. Jesus told His disciples that anyone desiring a place in the kingdom of God would need to demonstrate child-like faith.

If we teach our children that Jesus wants us to share with the poor, they will notice every poor person in town. Their eyes are open and they want to obey Jesus.

The harder part is teaching them to walk by faith. Children tend to walk by sight because the things that occupy their time and their minds are tangible and present. So learning a faith-walk will come largely from watching a faith-walk. They learn from others who choose to trust God and His word and walk by faith.

How do we do this?
- When possible share areas that you are learning to walk by faith.
    - Talk about trusting God with the weather and with traffic and schedules etc. God is involved in all of those areas. We can plan a picnic and pray for good weather, but if God sees fit to allow rain, we can teach our children that God had another plan for us that day and that His ways can always be trusted. If you are running late because you are behind slow drivers, you can explain to your children that you are trusting that God has allowed this slow car for a reason. You may not even know what it is, but you can trust God's plans. Of course talk about the positive evidences of God's hand at work in your life too, thanking God for the nice weather on the day of your picnic etc.
    - If you are considering a new job or have recently lost your job, talk about trusting God with His plan for your life. Pray together that God will make the next step in your faith journey clear. Not every step of your faith journey is appropriate to tell your child. (The goal is not to terrify your child with thoughts that there might not be enough money for food next week.)
- Identify areas in their lives that they need to trust God.
    - School – moving up a grade, moving up to a new building, difficulties with their studies or with teachers, not making a team, or losing an important game
    - Picking friends, choice of activities, time management
    - Family relationships and responsibilities
- Read Christian biographies

- This is a wonderful way to introduce your children to people who have lived trusting God in the midst of difficult circumstances. Watching other people exercise faith and then watching God demonstrate His faithfulness to them is an excellent faith-builder in our children's lives and in our own. There are many resources available from Christian bookstores. <u>The Trailblazer Series</u> by Dave and Neta Jackson is one resource as well as a three volume series they have written called <u>Hero Tales</u>. Another resource is a series of books for older children called <u>Heroes of the Faith</u>.

Anxiety and worry are faith dissolvers. People who respond to the unknown with anxiety and worry have their eyes set upon themselves and their own wisdom and strength to solve the problem. Faith, on the other-hand, grows strong out of hearts that are focused on Jesus, completely resting in His plan and His purpose. Children who grow up in homes filled with faith find great comfort in knowing that their parents walk confidently and peacefully after God. They learn the value and importance of trusting God to be their shield.

The Helmet of Salvation

Think more highly of others.

The helmet of salvation is one of the most difficult pieces of armor to put on. I think that is why it comes as the last piece of defensive armor. It is the setting aside of our old nature and its insistence that our needs be met—the "me, my and I" syndrome that plagues us.

In our children, this is their natural response, especially if they have not accepted Christ as their Savior yet. This is how they think because they have not been set free from the bondage of their old sinful nature. Even if they have accepted Christ, they are baby Christians, just learning how to walk, and that means that they will be stumbling and falling as they try to walk on their new spiritual legs.

It is important that we begin to teach our children how to think like Jesus as soon as we can, exposing and correcting their sinful thinking patterns and showing them how Jesus would have them respond.

The younger that we begin this "renewing of the mind" (Romans 12:2), the easier it will be for our children to esteem others more highly than themselves.

What types of things can we do in our homes that demonstrate to our children that we are wearing the helmet of salvation and that we want and expect them to desire to wear it also?

- Model this new way of thinking.
    - This is a very important piece of the puzzle. As our children watch us esteem others, they will recognize the value of others. What are some things that you can do to show that you esteem others?
        - Be patient as you wait in line behind people.
        - Do not honk at the car in front of you because they get a slow start on the green light.
        - Do not talk about people in a negative way.
        - Offer to give up your seat to elderly people.
        - Offer to help set up events at church and volunteer to help clean up afterwards.
        - Make a sacrificial gift to someone in need.
        - Make meals for the sick, elderly, neighbors or new moms in your community.
        - Of course there are so many other ways to model this, but as you consciously think of others and esteem them, your children will learn to value others also.

The Armored Baton

- Teach as you model.
    - This is important because we don't want our children to grow up focused on *doing* things for God rather than *being* who God wants them to be. Our service should come out of a life that has been fully protected by the armor of God.
        - We know the truth and we are following God.
        - Our hearts are set on things above.
        - We are obedient to the things that God asks us to do.
        - We walk in faith wherever he leads us
        - Now we live sacrificially for others, demonstrating the evidence of a heart and life controlled by the Holy Spirit of God.

The danger of our children thinking they can just *do* things for God is that they may never grow up *being* who God wants them to be. So teach as you model. Tell them why you are staying to help clean up or why you are bringing a meal to someone else.

In a culture that is very self-centered, this is a vital piece of the armor our children need to protect them from the lie that life is all about "me, my, and I." A child who never learns to walk in newness of life, under the control of the Holy Spirit, will never be ready to take up the sword of the Spirit and use God's Word to do the things that God has planned for them because their hands will already be full—of *themselves*.

Practice Philippians, chapter two in your homes, and your children will learn what it means to live in newness of life –wearing the helmet of salvation.

The Sword of the Spirit

Your words bring life and healing.

Teaching our children to use the sword of the Spirit is a little bit different than teaching them about the other pieces of armor because this is the only piece that is an offensive piece of the armor. The other armaments are for the protection of the person wearing them; this one is to be used to bring life and healing to people around them.

In many ways emphasizing God's Word is something that we have already been discussing throughout this short study on making sure our children grow up protected by the armor of God, but we need to note a specific slant to using the Scripture in an offensive manner; this time we need to point out the value that Scripture has in changing other people's lives.

When you parent and teach your children the Bible, you are actually using God's Word in an offensive manner. You are using God's Word to change the lives of your children. Be sure that as you use the Word of God to bring change and growth into their lives that you are modeling how to share the truth in love because now you will need to start encouraging your children to look for ways to share God's Word with others.

There will be many times in your children's lives when the opportunity arises for them to share God's corrective Word with their friends.

Suppose your child's friends are talking about cheating on a quiz or test. If you have already prepared your child to stand firm on God's Word, he/she will have the privilege of speaking up as to why that would be wrong and displeasing to God.

The list of possible scenarios is as endless as the list of mischievous behaviors that children get involved in.

One mistake we often make as parents is to encourage our children to tattle if someone is doing something wrong. Tattling is to be encouraged if the child is in danger of hurting himself or others; if there isn't any danger, then instead of teaching them to run to an adult to tell on someone, we can encourage our children to put Galatians 6:1 in practice: **Brothers, if someone is caught in any wrongdoing, you who are spiritual should restore such a person with a gentle spirit, watching out for yourselves so you also won't be tempted.**

A biblical response to seeing someone sin is to correct them gently, showing them why what they are doing is wrong. It is sharing God's truths with them and praying for them. It is okay to tattle on the person to God. He already knows what they are doing, and when you are tattling to God, you can pray and ask God to help the person to stop sinning.

The Armored Baton

You will have many teaching opportunities with your kids. They may come home from school with stories to tell of what they heard or saw and how they responded to it. Use the wisdom that God gives you to teach them the best way to respond.

Peer pressure can be a serious stumbling block for our kids, especially as they get older. Teaching them from a young age to respond to life's situations through the lens of God's Word and recognizing times when they can share that perspective with their peers is a great foundation which will help them during those sometimes unsteady teenage years when the pressure to do what the crowd is doing is at it's peak.

If you're thinking that your child might not be very popular with his peers if he corrects their sinful behaviors, you may be right. Teaching them to be sensitive to the Holy Spirit's leading is going to be important, but in the end, whether or not your child is the most popular kid in school or not, if they are learning to filter all their decisions through God's Word, they will be highly esteemed by God.

Isaiah 66:2 My hand made all these things, and so they all came into being. This is the LORD's declaration. I will look favorably on this kind of person: one who is humble, submissive in spirit, and trembles at My word.

Let's commit to being focused in our efforts to raise children who love God and seek Him with all their hearts. This goal won't be achieved without a purposeful plan and a commitment to seeing the plan to fruition. There will be many opportunities throughout your eighteen years of training to become distracted, discouraged, and quit. Don't do it. Stay focused, stay in close fellowship with God, seeking his wisdom and His strength and press on to your goal of having demonstrated to your children a life lived for God's glory.

As your children witness God's power and strength at work in your life, and as they have been taught by you to:
- Live by the truth of God's Word
- Set their hearts on things above
- Walk with obedient feet
- Keep their eyes on Jesus
- Live under the control of the Holy Spirit

They will be ready to take up the sword of the spirit

                         . . . and walk on their own, soldiers of the cross!

So run the course and pass the baton of faith on to your children. We need to be equipping them so that they in turn will be prepared to pass their faith onto the next generation until the day that Jesus comes!